LEADERSHIP BASICS

THE GUIDE TO LEADERSHIP, RETAINING TALENT AND BUILDING COMMITMENT

BY DR. EDWARD J SHELTON

Trafford
PUBLISHING

Order this book online at www.trafford.com/07-0934
or email orders@trafford.com

Most Trafford titles are also available at major online book retailers.

Note for Librarians: A cataloguing record for this book is available from Library
and Archives Canada at www.collectionscanada.ca/amicus/index-e.html

ISBN: 978-1-4251-2723-7

*We at Trafford believe that it is the responsibility of us all, as both individuals
and corporations, to make choices that are environmentally and socially sound.
You, in turn, are supporting this responsible conduct each time you purchase a
Trafford book, or make use of our publishing services. To find out how you are
helping, please visit www.trafford.com/responsiblepublishing.html*

*Our mission is to efficiently provide the world's finest, most comprehensive
book publishing service, enabling every author to experience success.
To find out how to publish your book, your way, and have it available
worldwide, visit us online at www.trafford.com/10510*

 www.trafford.com

North America & international
toll-free: 1 888 232 4444 (USA & Canada)
phone: 250 383 6864 ♦ fax: 250 383 6804 ♦ email: info@trafford.com

The United Kingdom & Europe
phone: +44 (0)1865 722 113 ♦ local rate: 0845 230 9601
facsimile: +44 (0)1865 722 868 ♦ email: info.uk@trafford.com

10 9 8 7 6 5 4 3

TABLE OF CONTENTS

They Love You – They Hate You is a real issue in leadership, some leaders would argue that they had rather be respected than loved, while other leaders view being hated as a indication of discipline and strength needed to move organizations forward. This book will dissect these leadership perceptions and address the general characteristics of hated leaders and beloved leaders. We will uncover why leaders are hated and why they are loved or admired.

They Hate Me	They Love Me
You are indifferent to the plight of those under you and may be the axe man, willing to sacrifice them in order to achieve your own ambition.	You care for those under you – you offer recognition and support and protection. People trust you.
You are mysterious and aloof, distant and unapproachable, you don't have much time and are always busy.	You are accessible, you are seen and heard. You do the unexpected.
You have many quirky ways that have no impact on the organization, such as setting rules that are unreasonable or self-centered.	You are courageous when it comes to defending your people. They seek your advice and opinions on personal matters.
You feel a sense of entitlement as a leader. You feel that your ideas are superior to the groups and do not trust them to accomplish the task.	You seek the groups input and ask for their support and are not afraid to delegate and place trust in them.

Why is being loved or hated important? Because, the relationship between leader behavior and follower commitment directly impacts the organization success. Recent literature suggests that followers who are committed to the organization are first committed to their boss's and the correlation is clear, they love their bosses while those who are not committed to their organizations do not respect and are on the verge of hating the boss. This correlation does have impact on organizational effectiveness and survival.

Impact on the Organization

In recent years, more companies have closed their doors or have merged at a faster rate than ever before. Most were successful thriving organizations on the cutting edge of their particular industry. Their leaders were decision makers; they were ambitious, they developed business plans, growing the organization with energy and drive. Yet their practices, values and knowledge could not guarantee them success.

Existing literature would suggest that these organizations experienced a typical life cycle of birth, growth, maturity and decline even to death. As this cycle matures, practices, values and leadership style shape the organization so that these dynamic creative forces become accepted and are rarely challenged.

Leaders become fixed in their actions, on the equipment, their investments and focusing on their success so much that they forget the most important asset they have, their people.

If your organization is undergoing tremendous success and there seems to be no ceiling, remember, it guarantees nothing for the future. Your success will hinge on how you develop your people, they will take you to the cutting edge and keep you their if you have the leaders who can inspire, develop trust and successfully get the people to participate in the entire process. It starts with effective leaders.

Let me share with you a few statistics that will help put today's leadership challenges in prospective: Many ongoing polls of employees find that

— Nine percent of Americans describe the relationship between management and labor at their organizations as "extremely positive."

— Forty nine percent describe their relationship as "lukewarm to negative."

— Ninety percent strongly felt that their organizations did not listen to or cared about the workers.

— Ninety percent do not trust their bosses to look out for their best interests.

If we can believe this study and other literature regarding leadership today, it suggests that 90% of leaders today lack the ability to motivate, inspire, and gain the commitment and respect of those who follow them.

Of the 90% of bosses who lack the ability to motivate, inspire and gain commitment, about 50% are considered abusive characterized by 6 traits:

1. Fail to keep promises.
2. Invade employee privacy.
3. Fail to give proper credit.
4. Blame others to cover up mistakes or minimize embarrassment.
5. Make negative comments about employee to other employees.
6. Give employees the silent treatment.

The major problem with having abusive or ineffective bosses is that employees don't leave their job or company; they leave their bosses. Most exit interviews at organizations with high turnover, (10% or more), reflect that the reason they are leaving is because of their boss. With this information in hand, it is hard to understand why organizations do little about it. Most recent polls of executives and presidents of companies, when asked which factor are the most crucial to the business, the top answer is always; retaining key workers and hiring qualified workers.

Retaining and keeping good workers is rated above all other concerns such as developing new products, increasing productivity, upgrading technology, expanding markets, finding new finance and cutting costs.

Faced with these statistics, you have to wonder where the disconnect is between leaders and the workforce, why are people leaving good paying jobs after years of training, time and investments? The answer can be found by reviewing the reasons people leave. The top three reasons are; first, lack of trust for their leaders, second, lack of recognition and praise and third, poor communications.

These findings are not new, top executives and consultants have acknowledged these problems for decades now. At the same time that top executives acknowledge that people are the most important assets they have, and that good employees are in short supply, why do they allow for those key leaders under them, effectively drive those very workers away?

The answer is both complicated yet simple, American workers want effective leadership. The complicated portion of this question has to do with the individual leader's behaviour and attitudes which of all assets within an origination, is the hardest to change and form.

The leader's practices and views define the organization's culture and the expectations of the organization in terms of employee behavior, customer service approaches' and other practices. The leader's constructed culture becomes ingrained in the organization, and often, over time the practices and values are not challenged or questioned, therefore, it becomes important to understand that leadership style does impact organizational effectiveness. Two ways to improve ineffective leadership styles and skills at this level or at any level is through self awareness leading to change or effective ongoing training by the organization.

The truth about leadership at the top and at the front line level is that although it is the heart of the organization, it is the least understood and mastered asset.

When there is emphasis on leadership development, it is often focused at the top tier, but seldom goes much farter down. Yet no matter how successful a leader is at the top, it means nothing if there are not effective leaders at the front line – in direct contact with the employees, who understand and share those same characteristics and abilities in proportion to their assigned responsibilities.

I was once part of an executive team tasked with developing senior people in our organization. We recruited top consultants to help design and build an elaborate program to develop our leaders. The fees for their work exceeded half a million dollars per year, not considering the lost time off the job of those who participated. After 18 months, a meeting was held with the president of the organization in which after two hours, the president rose from his chair, stating, "I can't see one change to this organization, no, not one."

The experience illustrates some flaws in this approach to developing leaders. The organization did its best, using the latest teaching methods to better its leaders and make a difference for those who participated. There were some short-term benefits, new ideas, critical thinking opportunities, and exposure to new tools. What the president of the organization saw, though, was that there was no evidence of permanent improvement in the organization or that the participants were better leaders than before.

The problem did not have its roots in insufficient effort or financial support. The problem was the relationship between the cost and the result. The president saw a disparity between what was being spent and the return on the investment, as result the leadership development training had not been effective. The top leadership had realized some benefits, but the benefit had not penetrated down into the organization, to the followers. One example cited by the president just before the meeting ended, was a statistic that showed skilled front line workers who were leaving had not changed.

In more than 25 years working with leaders in the military, in academic halls, and in business, I see the challenge facing leaders is the same: "How do we retain talent within the organization?'

To help answer this question, I would like to share an incident that happened many years ago, in another organization, as I was training a large group of front-line managers on leadership principles. This incident helps to underscore the earlier president's concern for effective training.

During one particular training session, I had just finished discussing the principles of motivation when a participating manager raised his hand and in all sincerity asked, "Have our bosses attended these courses?" There were a lot of laughs but a cord had been struck, I tucked that comment aside and did some checking. Sure enough, not one of their bosses had taken the leadership course they had mandated for all their subordinates.

A concept that I have taken from my military experience and one that can be applied to business is the philosophy, "Train everyone to lead." If every level is trained to lead, a hierarchical organization melts into a series of high-performing small units where change is managed with creativity and flexibility, and risk-taking can benefit the organization as front-line leaders are empowered to make innovative decisions.

Defining Leadership

To understand leadership at all levels, it is important to identify the fundamental differences between management and leadership and those principles that are essential for all leaders to understand.

Management is the process of planning, organizing, directing, controlling and coordinating resources that lead to achieving organizational goals. Leadership is more complex and involves relationships with people.

Leadership is more active, its interpersonal – true leaders inspire, have vision, set directions, enable people to extend their capabilities and ultimately inspire loyalty and command respect. Effective leaders tap into the followers' soul and have them choose to give their talents and commitment to the leader. These precious choices are not to be extracted through fear or intimidation but rather simple desire and free choice.

Understanding leadership dynamics requires first understanding the basis of social power that enables people to direct others.

Leadership entails boldness, venturing out to the cutting edge, leading from the front, and being susceptible to criticism. I imagine that everyone reading this book is a leader or has influence in the lives of others even if you don't realize it. My question to you and for you to seek out is what kind of leader are you or do you want to be? What kind of influence will you have on others?

My challenge to those in leadership positions at all levels is to view this book as a guide for leadership principles, understand and then apply them. You will find within yourself that leadership that is illusive to over 90% of leaders, it is what the academic world calls a transformational leadership style, perhaps the most powerful style available to mankind.

1

ROLE OF LEADERSHIP

If we believe that a leader's role is to inspire, have vision, set directions, and enable people to extend their capabilities and ultimately inspire loyalty and command respect. How is this achieved? Do we use fear as we have seen others do; or do we use kindness with a soft touch? The answer may surprise you.

There are many different techniques, principles and styles that can make a leader effective, yet allow for people to maintain their dignity and self-esteem.

No other story illustrates this better than from the view of a shepherd and the sheepherder.

The Good Shepherd

When I was a teenager in Italy, I lived near a field where a large flock of sheep grazed. Every evening, the sheep would be driven across the field and into the nearby mountain meadows for the night, by a man with a stick and his three dogs. As he walked behind the sheep, he would pound the stick on the ground driving the sheep forward, while the dogs yapped and nipped at their heels. If a sheep went the wrong direction, the man would strike the terrified sheep with his stick. He was a sheepherder.

In contrast, several years ago in Mendoza, Argentina, I saw a great leader. He was fourteen years old at the most, his trousers were torn, he wore no shoes, and he was playing a musical instrument traditional to that region. There he was, flute in hand, playing and strolling leisurely in front of a flock of sheep, and they were following him. Every move he made, they made; he went left, they went left; when he would stop, they would stop. As they drank from the stream, he counted them to ensure all were safe, and then he drank last. There was no other compelling force to drive them; no stick, no dogs – nothing. They knew who their leader was and they trusted him. I haven't seen such a dedicated leader since.

What was the difference between the shepherd and the sheepherder? It was leadership. Why does this apply to you? <u>Because, you are a leader.</u>

It is impossible for us to live in today's world and not be a leader. If you are a mother, father, family unit, social group or a direct leader at work, you will have responsibilities over others. Every time you consciously or unconsciously influence another person to make a decision, you are being a leader.

If you are a new leader, this book will help you construct a leadership foundation upon which you will build your entire life. And if you don't think you are a leader, please go back and re-read the last paragraph.

For the seasoned leader, you will recognize the power of the following principles found in this book. Hopefully you will commit to driving them down into your organization, especially to the front line leaders where they are often overlooked.

Leadership Is All About the Individual

It is important to understand how different styles of leadership affect those being led. Since you are dealing with people, not sheep, finding one grand theory of effective leadership that applies to all will be impossible. There will be as many different responses to your style as there will be people you are leading. And while there will always be scholars gathering and presenting their theories to explain this moving target – think "paradigm shift" – the truth is: Leadership is all about your relationship with the individual.

Effective leadership is the energizer from which human assets get their drive and productiveness, both on an individual basis and at the organizational level. This is especially true when working in a team environment. Human assets are simply…the people. Just as machinery, that is not maintained or is fed the wrong amount of energy, will break down or underperform, so goes it with your human assets. People – a much more important asset than machinery – need maintenance and attention, too, especially at the individual level. Unlike machines that work within a narrow, predetermined set of limits, people bring to the organization critical talents, skills, and precision that machines will never provide. The leader who ignores the importance of the individual loses the benefit of that worker's mental and collective potential.

It has been my experience that leaders who understand the value of the individual are in demand at all levels. Organizations recognize these leaders and their ability to manage change and tap into the knowledge and talents of the workforce. These leaders are able to empower and motivate others, and this then becomes the choice of style for the future: to focus on the individual, and jointly, the people. While there may be shifts in concentration and/or direction, it remains the most desirable style. Then, by harnessing the collective knowledge and talent of teams of people, any organization will be on the cutting edge of competitive advantage. Understanding and applying this concept of the "individual", requires that a leader make a contract between him and each individual, of which he must be prepared to mentally sign, agreeing on the terms from the beginning. The contract must express the importance that they each become mutually supportive for the good of both.

It can best be summed up by Edmond Burke in his letter, *Reflections on the Revolution in France* (1790). He stated,

"Society is indeed a contract. It is a partnership in all science; a partnership in all art; a partnership in every virtue and in all perfection"

Edmond Burke's comments provide a model for today's leadership; it is a reminder that the role of a leader is a partnership and moral contract that helps others to succeed. It is a race; not to win, but to achieve success for all. Achieving this partnership goal will depend on leaders developing in themselves and others a tolerance and understanding for differences in culture, for individual traits, and for organizational needs.

Five Principles of Partnership

In order to have a true impact on others, leaders must embrace the following five principles upon which the partnership is founded:

1. Knowledge Sharing
2. Trust
3. Empowering Others
4. Building Teamwork
5. Building Team Trust

1. Knowledge Sharing – Sharing knowledge enables an organization to harness the collective creativity, skills and talents of the workforce. It acknowledges the importance of everyone's role as a partner in the business, and helps develop strengths that build competitive advantage. With knowledge, people feel empowered. When sharing the vision of the organization with everyone, individuals can then be encouraged to identify the connection between their actions and the organization's goals. Once brought into that vision, they can see how maximizing their contribution to the organization provides value to all those affected, including themselves. To be effective, all knowledge must be passed down to the first line operators.

People must identify with the group or organization and have a personal and deep understanding of what is going on and why. Sharing knowledge tends to do away with the need for rewards for participation or for punishments for non-participation. When most knowledge is common, a team-like atmosphere is created. There is little or no separation between those who "know" and those who "don't know," creating a deeper bond between members of teams, and between teams and the organizational goals and objectives.

However, building cohesive teams requires that management empower each member, and the team as a whole, to affect change at the lowest level. Teams must also feel free to exercise their creativity, and be given the information necessary to drive those changes.

Studies show that leaders who empower their workers, and who lead others to lead themselves, are not afraid to redefine their own role with the people by building relationships. They call this management style "super leadership".

The relationship between managers and workers has been reshaping itself for several decades. In many organizations that relationship is seen in terms of coaching, mentoring, and facilitating, so the division between a manager's role and that of the worker may seem blurred at times. There is still purpose in defining the different roles, but the more current processes, which tap into the minds and knowledge of workers, give them more freedom to act independently. In some organizations employees are now in charge of tasks that once were reserved for management or specialists. This empowerment requires leaders who are able to foster a work environment and not fear encouraging employee participation in the workplace.

2. Trust – Trust is built upon the leader's integrity, ability and benevolence, and is an important aspect in developing and maintaining workplace relationships, and communicating vision, help to create the environment needed in order for empowerment to take place.

The importance of trust as a factor that defines empowerment in a workplace is becoming more diverse. It requires mutual trust to bring this diversity together in such a way, that workers of different cultures and backgrounds can feel comfortable working with one another and experience commonality.

The use of participative management styles and the emphasis on work teams have led to a focus on researching trust. The increased interest and reliance on teams and employee empowerment has increased the importance of trust as management control mechanisms are reduced and interaction increases.

Highly effective organizations are characterized by a horizontal structure where task-oriented groups gather to work together on tasks, rather than as a vertical command and control structure. To succeed, there must be trust built among the members of each group, including trust that each will carry his or her own workload equally, and help bear other's burdens with genuine care.

The most important level of trust is between workers and their immediate supervisors. This interpersonal trust develops over time and results from day-to-day interactions between the two. Trust in his or her supervisor enables a worker to become more innovative and satisfied with what they are doing, and thus less likely to leave the organization.

As trust is established or re-established, organizations depend on workforce empowerment as a way of increasing decision-making at the lowest levels. Leaders play a critical role in creating the proper climate for successful empowerment, and to that extent, contribute directly to the enrichment of the employees' role in the organization, and to enhancing their feelings of self-worth and sense of determination.

Trust is so complex and deeply integrated into the collective success of an organization and of the individual, that a leader who has difficulty in gaining the trust of people will also experience difficulty winning the trust of others such as customers or investors. The connection between members' trust and shareholder value is strong; employee commitment leads to positive growth and return on investment. Creating empowered workers begins with trust in leadership, and within the work groups themselves.

3. Empowering Others – Empowerment means giving workers at all levels the knowledge, confidence, and authority to make important decisions. Effective leaders involve their people in the business process, and this empowerment leads workers to an enhanced sense of self-efficacy (one's belief that they can make a difference through their skills and talents). It enables those around us to take an active rather than passive role at work, and inspires people to do more than they thought they could do. Leaders who empower their people have enough trust in them to share some of the decision-making, which allows them to grow individually. At the same time they provide benefit to the organization.

Ineffective leaders tend to hold on to control and power, preferring to do everything themselves. Effective empowerment can be difficult in organizations that have too much bureaucracy, and where many, if not all decisions are made only by those at high levels. These executives have worked long and hard to get power, and they will not give that power up easily – plus they're afraid that workers don't know enough to make decisions on their own. Restricting employees' participation in this way has an impact on their ability to trust the leader with whom they deal, as well as the organization as a whole. An effective empowerment strategy must include a tiered structure of decision-making that is well-defined and understood by everyone before being implemented within the organization.

Another key element in empowering the workforce is how information is made available to the members. Employees who have knowledge concerning the organization's direction will have ownership in proportion to the amount of information shared. Combining knowledge and information with participation strengthens employee empowerment by sending a message that the worker is an important asset to the organization and that their efforts make a difference.

A leader who understands empowerment and delegation will let the people do everything within their power. He or she will stand in the background as a coach, fixing responsibility and then when necessary, providing instruction on how that responsibility is to be met. It is a continuous cycle. Give them freedom to do their tasks, never criticizing, but praising success and encouraging efforts.

I firmly believe that if empowerment is done consistently, not only is a worker's job satisfaction improved and enhanced, but the level of commitment to the organization is increased based on the added individual attention given them by both their supervisor and other members of their teams. This strengthens the relationships between supervisors, co-workers, and other levels of management within the organization.

Let me share with you some tips in developing empowerment:
- Do not be afraid to delegate – then become a coach
- Make the task seem exciting, challenging and important
- Show others you have confidence in their ability
- Give and show loyalty to people and expect it in return
- Expect much from people and give much back
- Follow people's progress, hold them accountable while still giving praise and direction in a spirit of concern
- Allow people to change their work process
- Allow people to make decisions involving money

4. Building Teamwork – Your success as a leader largely depends on your ability to connect people to the organization so that collective knowledge can help drive organizational effectiveness. The development and use of teams allows organizations to compete in today's markets. Leaders in today's workplace must be creative; that is the base for change. It drives innovation and defines organizational effectiveness.

Driven to become more competitive, organizations have realized that the only way to achieve market advantage is to either lower wages, reduce material costs (meaning cheaper products), or design a more efficient organization.

Maximizing the individual worker is a strategy that can be built into a design for more efficiency. Workers today, are part of a group that is part of a larger social structure. Organizations can tap into a wealth of energy, experience, creativity and insight by accessing the collective knowledge and ambition contained within that group.

Research shows that 80% of Fortune 500 companies use teams as part of the operational process in their plants and processing areas. The popularity of teams with successful and reputable organizations demonstrates that this concept has become a strategic asset in today's business environment. It will become more refined in its design and impact, rather than diminish and fade away.

The best decisions are always made in groups – it takes more time – It is a difference between "we made the decision" and "I" made the decision. How can you fail?

Utilizing a team approach results in a paradigm shift in how employees not only are viewed, but are treated as well. Another factor contributing to demand for employee empowerment and teams is the changing attitudes of the workers themselves. Employees want to participate and become integrated into the business operations of the organization. Workers have come to expect empowerment and participation and, in fact, if they are not motivated to be a part of the daily operation, will eventually cause the organization to suffer.

Things to be considered when designing a team include work design, composition, context and process. Literature suggests that people perform better when they are given opportunity to problem-solve, make decisions, listen, communicate both within and outside the team, and deal effectively with conflict. This is all made more challenging by their diversity. Developing these groups takes a dedicated management team who can monitor and supervise, yet knows when to be flexible and to let the team develop on its own.

One characteristic of an effective team is the high level of commitment of its members both to the organization and to the team. The stronger the team's interpersonal relationships, the greater the mutual accountability amongst the team members. Setting high standards of behaviour for team members when dealing with each other, requiring honest yet respectful communication without fear of ridicule, accusation, or reprisal, can increase the level of trust, which is invaluable when creating and/or maintaining a good team. This eliminates finger pointing and fault finding, and leads to a greater sense of common purpose and commitment. Members respect each other and demonstrate mutual concern as each has the opportunity to grow, strengthening their level of trust not only in each other but also in the team system.

An effective team environment contributes to the organization in several ways. Perhaps one of the most important is through the role teams play in managing change. Most organizational processes impact many different people. Evaluating and identifying an existing process, or a new one, for its efficiency potential should include input from those involved. Using the team approach to change creates a venue for that input, and can lead to minimal resistance. In turn, that promotes more frequent process evaluations, allowing for perpetual fine-tuning of the organization.

Let me share with you an experience I had with teambuilding and a very good leader who understood the importance of it. While in Waco Texas, I worked for Ray Parma, a Complex Manager. Ray grew up in central Texas in a Czechoslovakian community where Czech was the common language. Facing the challenges of English as his second language, he developed a work ethic that took him out of high school, into the military as a paratrooper in the 82nd Airborne, and eventually on to a job at a local manufacturing plant. Ray excelled over the years as a general labourer, and eventually worked his way up to the position of general manager over several plants.

When I met Ray, what immediately struck me about him was his knowledge of the industry, his eagerness to learn, his lack of an inflated ego, and his deep regard for the individual worker. Over time he and I were able to develop teams from which Ray was able to solicit ideas, encouraging the workers to participate in the change process. He effectively harnessed the collective knowledge and talent of the organization through education, participation, support of ideas, and a show of interest and concern for what was presented.

Ray also took time out of his busy schedule to conduct ongoing meetings both with groups of managers and with groups of employees. He asked both groups for their ideas, and shared with everyone, updates on the latest changes affecting their operations (which also proved effective in short-circuiting the rumour mill). He especially encouraged the employee groups to participate in the exchange of problem-solving ideas, and because he believed in the importance of these exchanges, Ray patiently addressed every concern brought before him.

"We've got to find that man with the match!" became Ray's motto when meeting discussions turned to the subject of "putting out fires," an exercise that consumes so much time and energy. The search for the source of the fire inevitably led to such phrases as "we were told", "they won't let us", "they told us", but when Ray asked for a definition of "they" – the man with the match – the group realized they (and he) did not exist. Ray then turned the focus on identifying what actions each individual and/or the group as a whole could have taken, or could take in the future, to prevent the fire from happening.

Most people left those meetings feeling encouraged to participate more, knowing they were empowered to challenge processes that did not make sense, and to make changes. Ray drove fear out and accountability in.

Perhaps the most important element of Ray's success was that he led the way, not Human Resources, not a consultant, but Ray himself.

He essentially followed these rules:
- Inspire and motivate
- Delegate and trust
- Hold accountable and follow up
- Teach by example and principle
- Be generous with appreciation

5. Building Team Trust – Team-building requires accountability at the top, the middle, the front line, right down to the employee levels. The key is to accomplish team building without demoralizing the individual.

During one of Ray's departmental meetings, an employee (let's call him Joe) recounted the following story:

To do his job effectively, Joe needed to get under the product being built. This called for a creeper with wheels. Joe needed new wheels for his creeper, but his repeated requests to his supervisor brought no action. Frustrated, but still determined to have the tools he needed to do the job, Joe bought the wheels himself. They cost $6.00.

Ray's response to the story was to pull a $10 bill from his wallet and give it to Joe.

Soon afterward, Ray met with all the supervisors and shared Joe's story of the wheels. He didn't have to point his finger at anyone because every supervisor had experienced a similar situation. Using Joe's story as an example, Ray's challenge to the group was to accept accountability, to make decisions, and to take action at the time needed. He held them accountable; he empowered them to act.

Every meeting with the employees, supervisors or managers began with the presentation of a variety of real incidents followed by a good exchange of ideas. As problems surfaced, lessons were learned. In a way, Ray was not only holding each individual accountable, he had also begun assigning accountability to the teams as entities.

Over time the meetings became shorter as the complaints and concerns dwindled. The workforce became empowered and trust was developed between managers and employees. When I left the organization, Ray's plants were recognized as the most profitable, and best managed overall, in the region. With very little formal education, using what experience and his own innate sense of leadership had taught him, Ray exemplified how powerful and effective valuing individuals and teams could be. His results showed that an organization's greatest asset is its people.

Choosing Leaders Who Empower, Manage Change and Build Teams

One of the challenges to establishing and maintaining employee- participation programs is to provide clearly defined management and leadership roles. This needs to happen at all levels. Key ingredients to running successful programs are leadership, facilitation, and empowerment. Without clear, consistent definitions and guidelines, on which managers and leaders can base their style and actions, employee empowerment can become just an illusion, not a reality.

The question then arises: Just what are we asking of our leaders, and are they up to the task? We like to think that a trait of good leadership is the ability to handle change, but everyone brings different things to the table. So to answer that question we need to do the following:

1. Clearly understand the program's goals
2. Learn what it will take to get there
3. Evaluate the leadership style of each person filling the role, one at a time

4. Having determined what will be required of them, assess each one's strengths and weaknesses, identifying both the obstacles to and opportunities for their success

There are some effective tools for leadership development available on the market. They include the Multifactor Leadership Questionnaire, and Geert Hofstede's Value Survey Module. These instruments can help identify and develop effective leadership characteristics for you or the organization. Other methods include, 360 feedback programs, coaching, mentoring initiatives and well thought out succession planning.

Over the years and continuing today, leaders have been selected from the top down. The trend has been to select successful, task-oriented individuals. By placing them in leadership roles, the hope is that by example, their strengths will develop in those they lead.

But the very qualities that lead to success for the task-oriented person are those qualities that can inhibit their success at team leadership. They focus on the short-term task at hand, to the detriment of long-term thinking. They maintain control to improve their process, not recognizing any need to involve others or build alliances. Relying on consistency and order for their efficiency, they see open communication and consensus within a group as weaknesses. They perform their tasks best in the hierarchical style of management. They are comfortable with centralized power and control; with information, policies and procedures being dictated from the top.

This ingrained approach to management makes the task of establishing a team-oriented environment most challenging. Those in management positions resist sharing responsibility and control with their workers, missing the value of self-directed and empowered teams and individuals.

Changing a traditional organization to one that embraces the team environment requires leadership that believes in the value of the individual and the team; leadership that is prepared to devote the time and resources necessary both to build and maintain it. This is true at all levels of the organization. Then once that commitment is made, those in leadership positions must build teams of workers capable of taking an active role in developing the organization into a more efficient, competitive entity, able to change and grow to meet the demands of its industry.

Senior management considers effective leaders to be valued members who form work teams or groups that contribute to the organizational goals. To do this, leaders will need to be able to motivate and empower, and to establish trust at both the individual and group levels.

To motivate is "to provide with an incentive." Toward that end, the capable leader will seek to understand the individual, to know their needs and wants. Through this awareness, the leader can help the individual make the connection between reaching the team's and/or organization's goals, and thus, reaching their own.

With this connection made, the charge is to set high standards; challenging and encouraging everyone towards a level of performance and productivity beyond their expectations. In support of this, the individual team members can be coached and mentored, promoting innovation and nourishing creativity. As each member of the team is strengthened, so is the team.

The roles that empowerment and trust play in keeping everyone involved are critical. A leader engages his followers and gains their trust by conferring empowerment. This means sharing control of work tasks, and allowing everyone to participate in the decision-making process. As a team and its members gain momentum, their contributions must be acknowledged by allowing them to retain the power to effect change. Otherwise, the trust originally gained is broken and efforts to retain everyone's engagement in the process will be met with scepticism.

Another element of developing trust between a leader and the people is the leader's willingness to build and maintain communications in a way that is open and honest; sharing information, and avoiding at all costs, exploitation of a team and/or its members for the leader's own interests.

Organizations such as Southwest Airlines, Walt Disney Company, Google, and Wal-Mart value effective communications skills and as result have seen the value of a higher level of employee participation and have designed programs that encourage idea-sharing, bottom to top.

It is also easy to see why organizations and teams would flourish in such a participative environment, and to understand the benefit of empowering workers. Empowerment opens the organization or group to all the pooled talents and skills of the team. However, empowerment is not easy to establish because it is dependant upon the leaders psychology, values and attitudes.

Empowerment requires that a leader be secure in their own position, and not feel threatened by the loss of control implied by sharing it with others. (They would see it as a loss, rather than the gain that it is.) These leaders may represent as much as 90% of existing organizational leaders today.

Organizations moving forward will face the new challenges of emerging, competitive global markets, accelerated changes in technologies, less-predictable economic shifts, the increasing frequency of mergers and acquisitions, and a more rapidly changing workforce. To remain successful they will need to provide an environment that encourages everyone to participate in meeting the demands of change, and to create an integrated system of empowerment to achieve maximum benefit from all their people.

Leadership will be the key to breaking away from the more traditional, less flexible styles of management. An organization will need to have the kind of leadership that can imbed in its entire workforce the sense of a common strategic vision, and can encourage challenges to the status-quo. This is achieved through empowerment and knowledge sharing, resulting in heightened mutual trust in the process, the leadership, and the organization.

Teams are made up of Individuals

Once teams, empowerment, knowledge sharing and participation are understood, they can never be elevated above the needs of the individual. Maintaining individual consideration and helping to build the individuals self-esteem, should be the leader's first consideration. Treating all employees alike, as if one were no different from the other, is a tragic mistake. The leader who takes the time to build relationships with each of his or her workers will be in a position to better understand and evaluate each of their talents and abilities, some of which may not be seen otherwise.

It provides a more intimate knowledge of the workers' motivations, making the task of aligning the individual's vision with that of the organization more easily done. It also can give the leader a glimpse of the worker's shortcomings and failures, providing a base upon which to build a plan of remediation. And finally, giving the individual this kind of attention, accompanied by a greater exchange of information, achieves a higher level of trust and mutual respect.

Front-line leaders need to be able to stimulate followers' efforts to be creative and innovative by questioning their assumptions, and by getting them to approach old problems in new ways. By encouraging their workers to come up with and share new ideas and ways of tackling problems, a leader can help to facilitate the exchange of information, leading to a more involved and effective team of people.

POINTS OF DISCUSSION

If you were to draft a moral contract between you and your workers – what would be the three main themes?

If you were to draft a moral contract between you and your family – what would the main themes?

How did Ray Parma build trust between himself and his workers? In your opinion, did Ray have a moral contract?

What makes teams successful?

Why do teams fail?

2

SET THE EXAMPLE

A Leader Creates the Working Environment

Go to any workplace, and ask the employees, what they feel are the characteristics of **good leaders**, I can assure you that the list will include the following:

- Listens to my ideas
- Treats me with respect
- Values me as a individual
- Patient – looks past my individual quirks
- Gives me recognition and praise

Part of building these characteristics is the leader's ability to create a positive working environment. A common exercise I use when conducting training sessions with supervisors to help them understand how a working environment can be create, is to spend the first few minutes warming the group up, building a relaxed and informal mood.

Once I feel that the group has reached a level of comfort and are relaxed,

I will hold one hand up and announce, "Before we go any further, I want to make one thing clear."

I point out an attendee who has come in late, has a soda on the desk, anything to make a point.

"Mike, I don't appreciate members coming in late, make sure that it does not happen again".

As I pause for a moment, I observe the participants. Some are visibly shocked, others express disbelief and fear.

I then announce, "Okay. Mike, I apologize. I was only making a point."

I then asked the group, "What changed? Just a minute before we were all feeling good, exchanging ideas and really bonding, now there is no exchange of words, the air is thick with tension, so again, what happened, what changed?"

The answer is obvious. I, their appointed leader of the class, created an environment that was not conducive for the free exchange of ideas, but rather one of criticism and condemnation. I changed it in a matter of seconds. I would suggest that I lost some respect from the members of the class and perhaps some trust.

Leaders are Environmental Creators

A leader must be creative and value creativity in his/her followers. Leaders must be agents for creativity. Creativity allows organizations to be flexible, adaptive and reactive to change.

Good leaders know how to harness the collective creativity of the group. They know how to work with the followers in a way that encourages the open flow of ideas and communication in a positively-created, working environment.

Creating this type of environment can not be done through intimidation and fear; it must be through patience and the act of instilling within the group, a desire to participate.

There is a direct correlation between a leader who has positive relations within his or her group and effective communications, which can't help but to positively impact performance within the follower, as well as within the organization. Positive relations will foster intellectual stimulation, and an aura of feeling comfortable enough to question processes and business practices. It will also promote employees to feel like they are included in on decision making and changes. Their value for thinking is acknowledged as a valuable contributor to the organization.

Leaders create an environment in which ideas can flourish and see the light of day. To do this, leaders must be self-confident and have faith in themselves and others. People in leadership positions need a solid sense of self. It serves them well in times of turmoil, which inevitably await those who aspire to lead. The way people feel about themselves affects virtually every aspect of their lives. Self-esteem, which emerges from a sense of confidence, thus becomes the key to success or failure. In effect, effective leaders defy the law of averages and win because they expect success from themselves.

Leaders Must Believe in the Organizations Cause

A critical aspect of a work environment is the leaders' actions toward his workers and the just cause of the organization. This sense of righteousness to the cause will also strengthen resolve. Conversely, where the leaders do not believe in the virtue of their actions, they will lack commitment and will be hindered by self-doubt. Such uncertainty will be apparent to others, undermining the confidence of the followers and encouraging their opponents. It will contribute to eventual defeat and failure.

It is important for each leader to become convinced of the worthiness of the mission, on some deeply felt level. Even when the immediate objective seems questionable, the leader must find justification in some indisputable value, such as support of the nation's honor. Then, that conviction must fortify all of the leader's actions. When a leader exudes a quiet confidence, surety, and decisiveness, followers will be inspired and opposition will be weakened.

Often times, effective leaders are described as "strong," "powerful," "magnetic," and "charismatic." But whatever else they may be, they certainly are self-confident. From this confidence, leaders are able to mobilize and inspire individuals and groups to make their own personal dreams and objectives come true.

Leaders Encourage Creativity

Where only unquestioning obedience is valued, and where only strict adherence to rigid procedures is allowed, inflexibility and predictability are the consequences. It has led to the downfall of many organizations and small business enterprises. To succeed as a leader, or even to survive in a constantly changing and dangerous environment, creativity and adaptability are essential. This is where leaders must apply their foundational knowledge to the objective at hand and develop solutions; even in situations where there is no textbook answer.

Good Leaders are Good Followers

People everywhere are always looking for someone to follow or for someone to lead them. A leader is a person who goes ahead of others to direct or guide them or to show them how to do something. Leaders not only tell others what to do and how to do it, they also show them by example. Most importantly, leader's help others grow.

Employees look to their leader for direction as well as leadership. They listen to their words and observe their actions. Often workers will pattern how they treat others after the advice they are given, or they follow what they see a leader-type do.

Here are some questions to ask yourself:

- What can I do as a leader that will help those who I have influence over?
- How can I developing characteristics that will help me become a good leader as well as a good follower?
- What are some ways you are, or can be a leader in your home? In your community?

Each of us is a leader. Nearly every person at some time, somewhere, in some way leads another person or group. Our lives touch the lives of others, and we influence them whether or not we intend to. Our influence, which is different from that of anyone else, is our leadership.

Leaders do not always have to hold an executive position, or be part of the management team. The most influential leadership opportunities are at the front line; supervisor and team leader levels.

Since in one way or another nearly all of us are leaders, it is important that we learn to be good leaders. With good leadership skills, we can improve ourselves, help others, and strengthen our relationships with our friends and family members. As leaders, we can improve the organization and work harmoniously with other departments.

The value of good front-line leaders is that they help to create better line workers. Salesmen can sell more goods, managers can do better work, and the president or CEO's can make better decisions; inspire, train, supervise, motivate and do other important things that good leaders do.

We can develop the ability to lead if we will work at it. We need to prepare ourselves by learning the principles of good leadership through observing and studying the fundamentals, and then we must live these principles daily.

The model leader learns to follow perfectly. In order to become truly effective leaders, we must learn to listen, trust, build bridges, and follow. This requires that we learn to identify and follow good examples. We need to find leaders who:

- Study their trade and perfect it.
- Serve others and put their own needs second
- Have integrity and are honest
- Are slow to anger
- Are respected by others
- Teach others

Leaders Must Respect Their Followers; They Don't Have to Like Them

As strange as this may seem, leaders must have respect for those they lead but they don't have to like them. Disliking someone because of their personal lifestyle, poor manners or individual style, does not mean you have the right to shun, openly ignore, speak down, or insult them in a disrespectful manner. Respecting differences that you do not like requires characteristics that many leaders find hard to master.

Those characteristics include empathy, compassion and tolerance. Think about how many times your personal preferences had impact on how you treated those under your direction? The office worker who has multiple piercings, the gay worker, the red-neck tough guy; whatever the example, at one time or another we have let our prejudices show through our words or deeds, causing mistrust and caution. Putting misdirected personal opinions and biases aside is critical.

I witnessed an incident at a plant that helped me to realize how important respecting others affects our ability to be good leaders. I was attending a meeting with several hourly employees representing different departments in the plant. The plant superintendent was conducting the meeting and the company provided hamburgers with fries. Everyone eagerly began enjoying the meal except for Joe, a fellow worker who had brought his own lunch. I told Joe that we had plenty of food and was he sure he did not want some. One of the other workers said it must be Good Friday, to which the superintendent made the comment, "So you're a Catholic Joe. All you guys eat fish today." There was a chuckle from everyone, even Joe.

Sensing Joe's discomfort, I asked "Joe, if you don't mind, tell us a little about Good Friday, and what it means to you."

A little startled the employee began explaining the reason he has fish and why he sacrifice's something on that special day.

I encouraged it enough for all to understand that this employee held some very personal, sacred beliefs that were to be respected. "Thank you for sharing that with us, I didn't know that", I said, and we began the meeting. Leaders must respect employees and act to make sure that those under them feel comfortable enough to trust the leader.

Respect is perhaps one of the more important qualities leaders can have, because it means they genuinely care for those they lead. If they respect those they lead, they want to help them improve their lives; they are concerned for their needs and want to help them reach their goals. At all times and in all ways in our leadership responsibilities, it is through our respect for the individual that we can help others accomplish this goal. Respect is a powerful motivator.

Leaders make sure that followers understand the purpose of their work. The leaders help them to understand their part in the work and to gain a vision of their important responsibilities. We need to give those who are to follow our leadership the vision we have of the purpose of our work, and help them understand the roles they are to play.

Leaders Inspire Others to Follow By Choice

Highly effective leaders understand the principle of agency or choice. They create eagerness in their followers; they do not use force or fear. When we attempt to force anyone to follow, we are using power and authority that define the organization and not us as individuals. Commitment becomes in apportion to the force we use. If we use a large amount of force and intimidation we receive very little commitment and trust. If we are to lead in an effective, committed manner, we must allow others the freedom to choose.

Effective leaders let people know what is expected of them. It calls for honesty; we must let others know what we expect from them, and what they can expect from us. When we give them responsibilities, we must carefully explain their duties, the time involved, the meetings they are to attend, and what they must accomplish. It has been my experience that when people head in the wrong direction, it is because they did not have a clear understanding of what was expected of them.

Give People Tasks that are Meaningful and Challenging.

There are three things that a leader can do to keep motivation and performance levels high:

1. Give employees opportunity to perform meaningful, interesting and challenging work.
2. Provide positive feedback.
3. Autonomy to perform that work in a way that is relatively free and under the workers control.

Meaningful and worthwhile tasks help people feel needed. Asking people to do things simply to keep them busy usually does not accomplish good results. As leaders, we need to help our followers feel that what they do is worthwhile. When we lead, we must be certain that we do not infringe on the time of others by giving them tasks that are not necessary. However, everyone must recognize that at times, there are necessary but tedious tasks to be performed. All of us must be willing to accept these tasks as well as those that seem easier or those that will bring recognition and praise from others.

Often times when leaders do not delegate to their people, it is because they simply do not understand they have to be responsible both to the organizational purpose and to the people. Too often leaders are afraid to risk poor results or have mistakes made so they tend to hold on to responsibility or micro-manage their people. Workers who are micromanaged and have little control over the work they perform describe the work environment as stressful, the boss as overbearing and report a diminished sense of self-worth.

Leadership has an element of responsibility to help the people grow, not only to build the organization, but also to build and expand the workers and other emerging leaders. This should be a leaders purpose—to help our followers grow and gain experiences and success. This usually can not be achieved with a micro-management style. Growth will occur in an environment in which workers are trusted to carry out their jobs in ways they feel important and allow them the autonomy to make decisions.

Leaders do the Unexpected

An indispensable ingredient of a leader's success is an almost tangible self-confidence, which causes them to radiate certainty, composure, and authority, and breathe life into an otherwise dull situation. This also includes not being afraid to do unexpected, uncalculated acts on behalf of those who he/she influences.

Effective Leaders Respect and Value the Individual

One historical example of this component is reflected in the life actions of Abraham Lincoln. Dale Carnegie relates a popular story of Lincoln confronting General Grant, and Secretary of War Stanton, before the end of the Civil War.

Both men were bitterly criticizing Lincoln for his leniency that they believed was destroying the discipline of the army; they stated publicly that his disregard for disciplinary guidelines or "transactional style" would ruin him politically. Lincoln seldom let the critics get to him when making difficult decisions.

For instance, one incident occurred that so embittered the military and most northern citizens at the time, but is now viewed as a true act of compassion for the individual.

A soldier's mother visited with Lincoln pleading with him to spare her condemned son from the firing squad; her son was caught trying to make his way home. He was caught, court-martialed and sentenced to be shot. The widow explained to Lincoln that she had already lost her husband and three sons to the war, and this son was the last. Lincoln listened quietly and then produced a piece of paper instructing the boy to be released immediately to his mother.

The generals were appalled when they learned that Lincoln not only pardoned the widow's son, but also publicly declared, "I am unwilling for any boy under eighteen to be shot." Then, turning to his Secretary of War Stanton, Lincoln added, "I have never been sure but what I might drop my gun and run myself, if I were in battle. Anyway, I don't see that shooting will do him any good."

Lincoln had no hidden agenda, he spoke from his heart, he was not afraid to do the unexpected; he did what others were afraid to do because of fear of losing their power and positions. Lincoln led the public and nation in the direction he truly felt was best for them. As a result, he was admired by most and despised by others. His promises were kept, his integrity was never compromised, and leaders after him have seldom matched his humility.

Leaders Set the Example

Living in Central America, I had the opportunity to travel and visit some of the ancient engineering marvels of the Maya, Aztec and Inca civilizations and became interested in ancient ruins. There is a fascination with some ruins that have heavy weights on top of columns and cut stone; some hold all the weight while others have fallen and crumbled. Those that remain standing tend to stand because, over time, they have had to bear the majority of the weight on top. I feel that strong leaders have similar characteristics. They are committed and they are not afraid to share the weight with others, but we must first be willing to have the entire weight *on* our shoulder. The leader cannot ask of others what his is not willing to do himself.

As a leader, your every action is watched, picked apart, and judged. In essence, your head is always above the crowd. The greatest inspirations have come from leaders who set the proper example. They practice what they preach and ask nothing more of their followers than that which they require of themselves.

As an infantry platoon leader in Korea, I was assigned to duty on the DMZ, with very little leadership experience. Being forward deployed on the border, our soldiers had to be in top physical condition. Each day, my platoon would start the day at four o'clock in the morning with a three mile run. Each week ended with a twelve mile road march up a steep, Korean mountain dubbed, "Misery Hill."

When I first arrived and took over the platoon, the morale of the thirty-two soldiers was one of complaining, criticizing and poor performance. During the runs, no one was calling cadence or chanting the traditional Army cadence calls used to help keep the soldiers minds off of the discomfort of the runs.

Things were not much better during the weekly road marches up Old Misery. There was no interaction between leaders. During periodical stops, everyone, including the leaders, found their own plots of ground and either sat down or laid down. The only interaction between soldier and leader was when our Company Commander happened by and shouted out insults and threats to everyone. His presence brought fear to all who encountered his tirades and ranting.

One evening I was sitting outside our assembly area, thinking of what I could do. I asked a trusted NCO, Sergeant Evans, what he would do about the problem. His observation was straight forward and to the point.

"Sir, no one is leading. Sir, you need to set the example."

Kindly stated, he said – Take charge. No one was setting the example. I learned a valuable lesson:

Doing nothing is not leadership

I immediately acted. Each morning for the next month, I led the run, calling cadence and leading the chants as we ran. I then challenged all my platoon sergeants and squad leaders to prepare themselves to take turns leading the runs. In order to help prepare them, I decided that the platoon sergeants and all the squad leaders would participant in evening two mile runs without the troops, taking turns practicing different cadences and songs. We did this for several weeks. The results were amazing. Our runs became faster, the morale was high, and we had no one fall out or lag behind. The big difference was that we as the leadership group – were a team.

My second goal was to improve our road march performance. When I arrived, it was common to have at least seven to ten soldiers fall out and be picked up by the ever present, First Sergeants jeep. I noticed that during critical breaks, the leadership was sitting around taking care of their own sore feet or just relaxing.

I knew that the front-line leaders were the key to motivating the soldiers. I began a routine during these brief breaks of asking selected soldiers two questions each time we stopped. How were they doing on water and how were their feet doing? I had them take their socks off so I could see the condition of their feet. I would try and visit the ones who were really struggling and speak some words of advice and encouragement. No yelling, no criticism or condemning. The action had its intended results; I began to notice that the squad leaders began to check on their members at each stop and had them take their socks off, inspecting sore feet and suggesting ways to keep them free of blisters.

The power of example clearly had an impact resulting in improved performance, morale, and reduced injuries. Perhaps more importantly, it extended to the soldiers what they really wanted most, someone who really cared. Afterwards, there were no stragglers, no fallouts; everyone finished contributing to the success of the platoon.

A leader is a person who goes ahead of others to direct or guide them or to show them how to do something. Leaders not only tell others what to do and how to do it, they also show them by example. As leaders we must be willing to go further, carry a little more of the load, be willing to give the last cup of water to another, but we must always cross the line first and lead the way.

3

COMMUNICATIONS

Effective leaders communicate

Every employee focus group, 360-degree feedback session, opinion survey, and personal interview I have conducted over the years, identify one common problem within the workings of an organization – poor communication.

Effective leaders understand the holistic picture of communications and its impact on the organization. Communication is not a cold impersonal process; it requires a deep interpersonal connection with the people around. It requires acceptance of multi-sources; the follower, the customer, the superiors, and colleague. It requires a truly 360-degree assessment.

The real problem in business is that many leaders see communication as unnecessary, too time consuming, or they are just not good at it. That's because sometimes making decisions without communicating is easier to do.

What we need to understand, is that effective leaders who communicate well, do it in tones of support rather than loudness. They intend to be helpful rather than hurtful. They tend to use communication to bind workers together rather than to drive them apart. They tend to build rather than to belittle.

"Leaders use effective communications which are expressions of affection and not anger, facts and not fabrication, compassion and not contention, respect and not ridicule, counsel and not criticism, correction and not condemnation. Their words are spoken with clarity and not with confusion. They may be tender or they may be tough, but they must always be tempered."

Another challenge that leaders face in the workforce is to condition ourselves away from the cold, calculating, business mindset, towards developing feelings for our followers and understanding that we are dealing with people of responsibility and character; mothers, fathers, sisters and brothers. When we develop this concern for the condition of others, we then will communicate with them in a way they listen and feel appreciated. We will then, as good leaders, win their trust and commitment.

The right type of communication helps us to develop respectful relationships and ultimately build up our organizations, also building up those whom we lead.

Seven Principle's of Effective Communications

Seven effective communications principles that employees say they desire:
- Listen to my ideas and what I say
- Don't make unreasonable demands
- Communicate with us
- Encourage participation
- Show genuine concern for our issues
- Don't do only what he or she, the leader, wants
- Be sensitive to problems and needs at work

Listening is Not the Same as Hearing Someone

During my first week as Assistant Professor at Penn State University, I met with the president of the school who asked me how I was going to teach all the materials I had been given.

I replied, "I will teach in such a way that everyone will understand and no one will misunderstand."

He then asked me, "How do you plan to do that? I can't think of any tenured professor who has managed to accomplish what you're saying."

I really had not expected that response. I thought for a moment and replied, "Well, I plan to speak the truth, choose words that are easy to understand, avoid arguments, avoid offending, speak as kindly as I can and I plan to listen and hear what they say."

To my delight he said, "You may have a chance here. Not too many of my professors know how to hear by being good at listening."

"Listening is *not* the same as hearing. Leaders need to hear *and* feel what is being said."

Leaders must learn to become good listeners. Leaders create an atmosphere of understanding and acceptance that makes people comfortable, because they listen with a patient ear and take the time to listen to and understand their people's needs, thus demonstrating true concern.

A different but effective way to listen to people is to let people think through their own ideas by asking them questions. This helps them understand what points need to be made. To be good leaders, we must help people solve their own problems and meet their own challenges. We can ask them questions to help them consider possibilities for resolving problems and guide them through the process.

Take time to listen – See Things from the Other's Point of View

At a processing plant I worked at, the plant manager approached the payroll manager and asked her why the payroll was recently incorrect. He went on and blasted her; questioning how he could trust anything she produced because of the recent errors, and on and on.

His parting words were, "I don't care what you have to do, get it fixed, now."

The plant manager failed to take the time to listen and hear her reasons; much less care about what she was struggling with. This manager was a competent, able, payroll manager with many years of success behind her. Now she was unmotivated, her self-esteem damaged and she began questioning her willingness to continue on with the organization. The plant manager did several things that were destructive: First, he did not take the time to hear the manager's point of view, and second, he failed to see the issue from the manager's point of view. As leaders, we must take the time to hear people from a 360 degree view.

"No Excuses" Leadership

We have too many leaders today who coin the phrase, "no excuses"; which I have never understood. Making such a dead-end statement cuts short any communication that might prove useful to both parties. Too many leaders do not realize the damage they do with their form and style of communication. They see condemnation and tough talk as a sign of power and strength. These leaders as well as all leadership must recognize the power of positive, effective communication and practice it daily. By applying good communication skills, we become better leaders and find greater success. Our communications are at the core of our relationships with others. If we are to expect commitment, performance and trust, we must develop trusting relationships with our employees.

Our communication reflects in our integrity and ability to be trusted. Therefore, we must be careful not only *what* we communicate, but also *how* we do so. People can be strengthened or shattered by the message and the manner in which we communicate.

We must express confidence in others and motivate them to find solutions and make decisions. New, emerging leaders within the organization often times find it very difficult to make good decisions all the time by themselves, but are not inclined to ask for help because they do not want to be seen or perceived as incapable. Leaders can find courage and strength in the help of others.

Avoid Destructive Communication

There are certain kinds of communication which destroy relationships and are not for our development but rather, our destruction. They result in diminished, opportunity and motivation. One of the major ways to destroy a department or division is for front-line leaders to participate in, or allow the use of gossip, rumor, and slander.

Perhaps the four most common destructive forms of communication are those of lying, blaming, criticizing, and anger. Leaders not only stop this type of communication, but they must set the example and not engage in it.

Lying

The first of these forms of negative communication is that of lying. To lie is to be untruthful, deceptive, deceitful, and dishonest. This is a basic communication problem which is not new; but always has the same results. It will destroy a leader's integrity and trust. Integrity is the core of our character. Without integrity we have a weak foundation upon which to build other leadership characteristics.

Blaming

A second destructive form of communication is that of blaming. This is a condemning communication. It is interesting that when people are afraid to accept accountability, they begin to place the blame on others. It has been my experience that weak leaders tend to blame mistakes and problems on others or on certain circumstances. When we attempt to place responsibility for our choices on others, we are responding in a leaderless manner.

More importantly, do not allow those under you to fall into the habit of blaming, encourage them to seek root causes.

Criticizing

A third destructive form of communication is that of criticizing. Positive or constructive criticism is feedback given with the purpose of helping another person to grow and to develop. This is both helpful and needful and is generally accepted and appreciated.

Negative criticism is intended to hurt and often to defame and to destroy. This caustic communication is cruel, and it tends to crush the character of all of those about whom it is directed.

Anger

A fourth form is anger. This is perhaps the most common form of destructive communication. Anger causes anguish to everyone who experiences the feeling, as well as to those who are the recipients of this emotional explosion. I have an expression I have used in my family when angry words are exchanged or tempers flare, "the sprit has been sucked out of this home." This term describes bad feelings and a breakdown of communication that destroys any enthusiasm or eagerness.

Anger shows a lack of self-control and an inability to relate in a professional way to others. It is a senseless substitute for self-control. It is sometimes used as a selfish strategy to gain control of a relationship.

"The moment a leader becomes angry they show a great weakness."

Effective leaders view communications as a tool intended to be helpful rather than hurtful. Communications can bind us together rather than drive us apart and it can build our employees rather than belittle them.

Leaders never Criticize, Condemn, nor Complain

I am convinced that most front line leaders do not understand the principles about personal criticism, especially the criticism of their followers.

I do not refer to the kind of criticism the dictionary defines as "the act of passing judgment as to the merits of anything." (*Random House Dictionary,* unabridged ed., s.v. "criticism.")

That kind of criticism is inherent in our freedom of speech and seeking truths. In the political world, critical evaluation inevitably accompanies any knowledgeable exercise of the cherished freedoms of speech and of the press. In the private world, we have a right to expect critical evaluation of anything that is put into the marketplace or the public domain. Sports writers, reviewers of books and music, scholars, investment analysts, and those who test products and services must be free to exercise their critical faculties and to inform the public accordingly. This kind of criticism is usually directed toward issues, and it is usually constructive.

The criticism that leaders must avoid is the act of passing severe judgment;

censure; faultfinding. Faultfinding is the act of pointing out faults, especially faults of a petty nature. It is related to "backbiting," which is attacking the character or reputation of a team member. This kind of criticism is generally directed toward a person or persons, and it is generally destructive in nature.

We are all prone to see the limitations and the weaknesses of our employees and our boss's, yet there are leaders who find fault and always criticize in a destructive way.

There is a difference in criticism. If we can criticize constructively for the true purpose of helping better the person or the situation, we may change beneficially and properly some of the things that are being done. But if our purpose is for faultfinding, of pointing out the weaknesses and failings of others in a destructive manner, our leadership will be dismissed and rejected by those who follow us, making our efforts futile. It can be one of the most un-motivating experiences.

I am not suggesting that leaders not be critical. Growth comes of correction, strength comes of change, and effective leaders are those who can acknowledge mistakes pointed out by others and knowledgably change their course.

What I am suggesting is that leaders turn from the negativism that so permeates our workplace, and look for the remarkable talent among those with whom we associate. That we speak of our employee's strengths more than we speak of their faults.

I have often heard department managers say, "I'm speaking my mind and telling you the truth."

The fact that something is true is not always a justification for communicating it. I maintain that a man who speaks his mind has poor judgment, specifically, there is "a time to speak," and there is also "a time to keep silence." Effective leaders know how to apply this principle.

As a leader, truth exists as an absolute, but our *use* of truth should be disciplined by other values. For example, it is wrong to make statements with the intent of harm or to gain advantage, even if the statements are true. It is wrong to threaten to reveal embarrassing facts unless a favor is done, even if the facts are true. We call that a crime of blackmail. Doctors, lawyers, and other professionals are forbidden to reveal facts they have received in confidence, even though those facts are true.

Truth is powerful and absolute in its existence, but its communication should usually be guided by companion principles. Leaders who use the sword of truth, might not be used to build their followers, but might be misused carelessly to embarrass, debase, or deceive others. The sign of an effective leader is often *silence*. Some truths are best left unsaid. There is not a better sign of good leadership than the leader who allows an employee to save face and move on.

A leader, who focuses on faults though they may be true, tears down those under him. The virtues of patience, kindness, mutual respect, and loyalty, all rest to some degree on the principle that even though something is true, we are not necessarily justified in communicating it to any and all persons at any and all times.

The use of truth should also be constrained by the principle of unity and team work. A leader, who focuses on faults, fosters dissensions and divisions among fellow members, splinters any hope of real, team participation and the establishment of trust.

Avoiding destructive personal criticism does not mean that leaders need to be docile or indifferent to defective policies, deficient practices, or wrongful conduct in the organization. Leaders should not avoid constructive criticism of such conditions. The leader should avoid personal attacks and shrill denunciations. Our public communications—even those protesting against deficiencies—should be reasoned in content and motivating.

Case – Don't Slap the Dolphin

When I lived in Orlando Florida, my best friend was a trainer at Sea World and invited me to watch one of his training sessions. The day came and my friend began his training session with the dolphin's swimming the perimeter of the pool then performing small jumps and finally spectacular aerial acrobats and twirls. The discipline was unbelievable and the skills these animal's possessed was spectacular. I learned that it cost nearly half a million dollars to properly train one dolphin and what they learned was for life as long as they were properly trained and nourished with the right foods.

At the end of the training session, my friend invited me to take a tour of the holding pins and veterinarian facilities. During the tour, I noticed a medium sized pin with a dolphin alone, by himself. I asked my friend why he was separated from the others. He explained that this particular dolphin was being prepared to be released back into the ocean the following day because he could no longer perform. My next question was obvious, – Why?

Several weeks earlier, a group of college interns were learning how to train dolphins; part of the training was behavior conditioning through rewarding proper behavior with rewards such as fish and squid. The process requires a trainer to either throw the fish into the dolphin's mouth or let it fall into the mouth just before the dolphin reaches the trainers hand. During the process of feeding the dolphins in this manner, one of the interns held onto the fish too long and the dolphin delivered a painful bite the intern's hand, leaving a nasty cut. Without giving it much thought, the intern reached down and as the happy, chattering dolphin appeared for another tasty morsel, the intern delivered a hard slap to the dolphin on its head.

The result was immediate and tragic. My friend explained that when a dolphin becomes offended or attacked by the one he has trust in, that dolphin will never perform again and will go to the bottom of the pool, surfacing only to get air but will never perform again.

On my way home, I thought about the dolphin that had been slapped and refused to perform again. I couldn't help but compare it to how people react with criticism and mental slaps, very few people really perform afterwards. I learned a valuable lesson – ***Don't Slap the Dolphin***.

Leaders Should Look for the Admirable Qualities in Their People.

When leaders look for the admirable qualities in their people, they are better able to prevent difficulties. They are also able to work together to resolve difficulties that arise, communication becomes welcomed and revered, and constructive advice is accepted and barriers are lowered.

While working in a poultry processing plant in Arkansas, the plant manager came to me to express grievances against his night superintendent. He was very critical of the supervisor and lashed out at his poor performance and attitude, which was getting worse.

After several minutes of listening to the manager criticizing him, I asked,

"What qualities did you see in him when he was hired, if you consider him so incompetent and reckless now?"

The plant manger thought for a moment and said, "Well, I suppose he had some good qualities, but I can't remember any. He must have changed."

I suggested that he take some time to cool off and try to remember the characteristics he had once admired in this superintendent. In a few weeks I asked him how the superintendent was doing. With a sense of excitement he stated that he had remembered some of the superintendent's admirable qualities. Before, he had been so consumed with seeing his faults that he had failed to see his good qualities.

Leaders, learn to listen, and listen to learn from your people. Taking time to listen is essential in keeping the lines of communication intact. If people are an important asset to your department or organization, they deserve prime time! Yet less important agendas and projects are given priority, leaving only leftover moments for listening to your people.

Conducting regular meetings to discuss problems openly and calmly, at all levels, are essential to knowing your people. Discussions should be conducted in a respectful way, without loud arguments or contention. The best organizations I have been part of had one common thread; they held daily department meetings and monthly plant/organization meetings.

While serving with a management team in Waco Texas, our team, under the leadership of Ray Parma, seldom had trouble, because there were hardly ever raised voices and arguments in our weekly meetings, Ray insisted that our communication be respectful, and as result, there developed a genuine respect and working relationships among the members. The key? Ray set the example. It is only when we raised our voices that the sparks flew and tiny molehills become great mountains of contention. When those few times happened, Ray quickly stepped in and did not allow it to build for very long.

Communicate in positive ways.

"In what ways do expressions of appreciation and recognition influence a relationship between leader and follower?" I have asked this question many times as I facilitated leadership training and in every case I hear:

- I am more committed
- I want to do well
- Improves communications within our group
- I enjoy coming to work
- I feel motivated

Ask your group this question. "How does negative communication from me—such as criticism, and fault-finding—affect our relationship?" Some popular answers are:

- Generally I am painfully aware of my weaknesses, and I don't need frequent reminders from you.
- I have never changed for the better as a result of constant criticism and condemnations.
- What my boss offers as constructive criticism is actually destructive.
- What kind of results do you expect from constant complaints or criticism?
- I hate when my boss compares my weaknesses to the strengths of others.

Let me share with you an incident that happened at a company I was working at. The owner of the organization was "intense"; a word that he liked to use to label himself, perhaps because he felt that strong leaders had to be intense with people. In one of our daily meetings just before Christmas, he was reviewing the events as they would happen. During the meeting a production manager was hesitant in giving answers, only because while he knew things were fine, he did not want to say something that was a bit off; he knew the owner was an intense man.

After the meeting, the owner pulled the production manager aside and asked, "You seemed a little uncertain in there, what's going on."

His tone was condescending and negative, his body language showed signs of disgust and anger.

The owner's intensity was actually negative communication which had a devastating effect on those around him. There were few who felt they could be honest and candid, essentially denying the president of much needed information and insight. While the owner saw intensity as positive leadership characteristic, it literally shut people down.

This is not a major example of an explosive boss, but it is a common example of how leaders can create a fearful communication style and never really understand how it impacts those around them.

This particular leader honestly felt that his style was effective, in fact he would label it as intense, pushing hard, and directing, in reality he was shredding people's self-esteem and destroying their trust and respect for him as a leader.

Learn to Give Honest and Sincere Praise

"A kick in the pants is just a few inches from a pat on the back – yet the results are miles apart"

People crave sincere appreciation; it is a reoccurring theme wherever I go when I ask employees, teachers and leaders themselves, what motivates them. As leaders we can focus on what employees do well, or what they do badly. I would suggest trying to focus on the good things those around you do, and let them know.

Giving praise is not a weakness nor will it make people soft. It is high on the motivation list. Let me list a few ways to deliver praise.

First, praise must be genuine and factual. It must be presented then followed up by an example. "Mary, I appreciate your hard work. The report you turned in helped the plant manger better understand our position in the market." Or "John, I appreciate you working on the ground beef grinder, you know it cost us a hundred-dollars-a-minute when it's down, you've saved us a lot of money."

This also goes for behavior. I have told employees who have made mistakes things such as, "I am glad you admitted the problem, it took courage to do that," and, "I admire how you handle difficult customers, it makes a difference when you are firm yet understanding."

Secondly, follow a compliment with a question such as, "The yield on your machines was great this month, how do you keep them running efficiently?" Putting a question on the end allows people to explain their skills and talents not simply leaving them not knowing how to respond.

Another good idea is to personalize the praise using their name. It demonstrates that you know them, and gives people a sense of importance that has a bonding effect.

Finally, give praise when the person isn't immediately around; such as during meetings, group sessions or to their immediate supervisors. Praise that is passed on to the individual has a powerful, self-worth affect. Giving praise tends to drive out fear from a group and creates an atmosphere of eagerness and gratitude.

4

TRUST AND RESPECT

Effective Leaders are Respected and Trusted

Leaders have to learn that the interest of their people is their own interest, or they will never build effective teams in today's organizations. Truly effective leaders are trusted and respected by the people they lead, they are admired for their honesty, concern and personalized attention to them. However, it is not given easily; it has to be earned by the leader through example and "walking the talk."

Trust building begins with the individual; building relationships will lead to workers who try harder, volunteer readily and eventually become committed to the organization. There are three ingredients to building the foundation for trust:

1. Ability
2. Integrity
3. Benevolence

These are the main factors that contribute to trust building. Trust is the willingness of our employees or those associated with us, to take risk, and the level of trust is an indication of the amount of risk that they are willing to take. It can be stated another way – Trust can be defined as a willingness to be vulnerable to their leader and is formed by the three factors of ability, integrity and benevolence.

Ability is the degree to which, we as leaders follow through on what we say, what we do and how it is done. It is the quality of our efforts compare to results we achieve. If we tell people one thing, even with good intentions, but do not have the authority or power to carry it out, then our ability is questioned and becomes degraded.

Integrity is who we are and how we are viewed by those around us based upon our history and interpersonal exchanges, it defines us to others. "If he says he will do it, he will," "be careful, he has a gambling problem," it is our ethics and values as seen by others and is the fabric of which we are made of.

Benevolence is the extent to which we are believed to want to do good for others interests. It is our degree of goodness within us to share and to help others. A good leader demonstrates that he or she considers their people's needs above and beyond their own. The leader represents their people's needs to higher authorities effectively, and does not let his or her own ambition interfere with what is best for them; even if it risks the leaders own interests. It requires the leader to demonstrate consistent application of ethics and principle.

Benevolent leaders are willing to give more to others than they receive

An element of benevolence is the ability to be kind. Kindness is the essence of greatness and the fundamental characteristic of leadership. Kindness is a passport that opens doors and fashions friends. It bonds people and molds relationships that are important to the workforce. The things that are important to us and ones that we remember most are the small acts of kindness that have been extended to us.

The power of kindness and its impact on people reminds me of a time when I was away from my family working in Colorado, a late winter storm tore through Texas falling limbs and debris. Our property was a mess having several large oak limbs lying around and it appeared that it would be months before I could clean up the fallen limbs. Several days after the storm, my wife called and told me that our good friend Dr. Stan Fowler had dropped by and cleaned up the storm debris. I was not surprised when my wife told me.

Dr. Fowler and I first met while working in Plainview Texas, he was the USDA lead Veterinarian and I was the HR Director at a large beef slaughter plant. When I first arrived at the plant, Stan was the first manager to introduce himself to me and went so far as to invite me to his home for dinner. His acts of kindness were welcome and continuous. Years later when I moved to Waco Texas, I was happy to run into Stan again, and to find out that he lived nearby. So when a storm came and without solicitation or asking, Stan showed up to help unannounced, it was not surprising. I knew that he was genuine about his eagerness to help; he had done it so many times before. What leaders like Dr. Fowler instill in others is a great desire to give back, to help and to return what has been given us. I'll never forget his kindness

The power of kindness should not be limited to outside our work. There is great power in benevolence that can benefit our workers. The attributes of thoughtfulness and kindness are inseparably linked with the principle of benevolence and trust building. Kindness is the essence of an effective leader. Kindness is how a person treats others. Kindness should permeate all of our words and actions at work. There is no substitute for kindness at work.

As a leader, the things you say, the tone of your voice, the anger or calm of your words—these things are noticed by your workers. They see and learn both the kind and the unkind things we say or do. Nothing exposes our true selves more than how we treat one another in the workplace.

I often wonder why some leaders feel they must be critical of others. It gets in their blood, I suppose, and it becomes so natural they often don't even think about it. They seem to criticize everyone—the way the secretary makes calls, how an associate needs time off to take care of family issues and more.

Even when we think we are doing no harm by our critical remarks, consequences often follow. I am reminded of a boy who handed an envelope with twenty dollars to his father's boss at a company fund raising event, and told the boss it was for him. The boss told the boy to give the money to his secretary who would forward the funds to the organization's designated charity, he explained to the boy that he should mark on the envelope what organization the money was intended for. The boy hesitated for a moment, and then insisted the money was for the boss himself. When the boss asked why, the boy replied, "Because my father says you're one of the poorest bosses he ever had."

One way you can measure your value as a leader is to ask, "How well am I doing in helping others reach their potential? Do I support others in the organization, or do I criticize them?" If you are criticizing others, you are weakening the organization. If you are building others, you are building the organization or department.

Importance of Trust

Leaders not only trust their followers but are trusted by them as well. They are not afraid to share responsibilities or teach them higher skills that require delegating and empowering others, giving them important things to do for their development. These leaders do not feel that they have to do it personally in order to get it done right; they are eager to share responsibility as a teaching opportunity for their followers benefit and growth.

A true leader sees followers not for what they are now, but for what they can become. I have witnessed excellent, young, managers and workers walk away from organizations because they were seen as too inexperienced to handle the job.

While working in the swine plants of North Carolina, my HR team put together an intern program designed to attract college graduates in preparation for filling future manager positions. One of our goals was to prepare future leaders by exposing them to real experiences under careful monitoring and coaching. We developed a program that would expose them to a variety of positions that included company farms, accounting, Human Resources and safety.

The experience was a win-win situation for both the student and the company. The important aspect of this program was the amount of trust given to these relatively, inexperienced, college students. In return, they were eager to meet the expectations set before them, and appreciated the personal attention showed each one. I realized that what made this program so successful was the mutual trust and respect developed due to the face-to-face, one-on-one exchanges that had developed. It was personal, caring, and not just a passing "hello" at the water cooler.

Our intern program was highly successful because it not only provided a good training vehicle to upcoming talent, but it sent an organizational message that said we cared, and were interested in our people's development and growth.

When developing these relationships, it is important to remember that it takes time and commitment to the individual, but over time you will realize better performance and behavior.

Good Leaders Hold Followers Accountable – Accountability is not the same as punishment.

There is no greater act of respect for others than to hold them accountable. I am amazed at how many front-line supervisors are afraid to hold people accountable. They are afraid that moral will go down, that relationships will be strained, or that they will be perceived as hard and unreasonable.

The fact is that accountability is the ultimate demonstration of a leader's eagerness to build and uplift their followers. If done properly, it gives direction, corrects dangerously developing patterns, and helps to stretch people up and into new horizons. Accountability is a major change agent; without it nothing improves, processes become routine, and growth suffers. The greatest lessons I learned as a young leader were when I was made to account for my failures and successes.

When a leader understands accountability, what they will soon realize, is that it is the ultimate demonstration of a leader's eagerness to build and uplift their followers.

I learned this principle early in my career as a Company Commander in the Army, stationed in Panama. I always insisted that my platoon leaders insure each soldier carried three days of water, food, and clothing; regardless of our mission's duration. I knew it was tempting in the tropical heat to lighten the loads, discarding items deemed unnecessary. I made it a policy that before each mission into the jungle, I would conduct a brief inspection on one or two of the soldiers.

If I discovered a light ruck-sack, I would call the Lieutenant aside and ask, "Lieutenant, help me understand why Private Miller's canteen is empty?", or whatever else was not in compliance.

I did it in private, with a calm demeanor, no barking in anger; I was holding them accountable.

As a result, our unit was a top performer. There were no injuries, everyone came home, and most importantly, the soldiers became better at what they did. They grew professionally and in the end, recognized that holding them accountable made them better individuals.

"Accountability is the ultimate demonstration of a leader's eagerness to build and uplift their followers."

Effective leaders understand how to hold members accountable without condemnation or excessive criticism. Leaders hold the followers accountable, not only for their actions, but for their development. Many well-meaning leaders protect their followers by withholding challenging assignments in order to avoid conflict or failure. Accountability is essential for individual development and change; it is extremely important that we set and communicate high standards. I have found that our followers tend to perform at a standard set by the leader. Where neither responsibility nor accountability is expected, growth and development stop.

The military places the concept of developing trust and confidence in its leaders, as one of the cornerstones for successful leadership. It has a field manual, FM 6-22, that suggests it's leaders continually develop their subordinates to improve their skills, keep them upward mobile, and help them become critical thinkers regarding all aspects of their mission.

They do not simply want a warm body that can carry sixty pounds on their backs and move from point A to point B in mechanical fashion. Rather, they want followers who can not only perform physically, but can also use their minds and creativity to be flexible, so that the unit as a whole may benefit. As a result of developing the whole individual, military leaders often times realize the highest levels of commitment and trust from their troops.

Setting High Standards

Setting and maintaining high standards of performance and conduct are other elements of accountability. It's okay to expect high standards from your followers. Setting high standards, both moral and technical, is a motivating experience that allows them to accomplish more than we thought was possible. This instills both individual and personal pride. Expressing and setting high expectations of performance, demonstrates a strong confidence in peoples' capabilities which inspires achievement for higher performance. As a result, there will be a desire for affiliation with the group who is number one.

A leader who does not set standards for his followers, condemns them to mediocrity and self indulgence.

Trust is Long Term

The value of establishing trust is that it lasts a long time. It stands the pressures of every day trials and adverse events. The more authority and trust you share with front line leaders, the more efficient the organization will become. I noticed that once I restricted or took away authority, the level of performance and commitment diminished with it.

Effective leaders know their followers, and seek their follower's best interests above their own.

During a training session with some managers in Texas, a manager asked me the following questions:

"What are your goals? What do you want to accomplish?"

I observed his seriousness of purpose, and answered in the same spirit, "My strongest desire is to qualify to be a friend of those whom I lead."

Good leaders are not afraid to be friends with those they lead.

I had not responded to such a question in just that way before, but the answer I gave, did put into words my deepest beliefs and yearnings. Most of us are committed to our true friends, yet we are afraid to extend that commitment beyond the bounds of our private lives.

I maintain that good leaders are not afraid to make friends of their employees, a concept that raises eyebrows in the corporate world. The problem is how friendship is defined and viewed; friendship is not the same as participating in destructive indulgence and the feeding of appetites and passions.

The dictionary tells us that a friend is a person attached to another by respect and affection. A true friend makes sure that your interests are protected. Leaders can create a more inspired and committed following if they understand the individual worth of each follower, and also understand the needs and individuality of the followers. Therefore, great leaders are not afraid to make friendships with their followers and to use friendship qualities to protect and develop them.

"I destroy my enemy when I make him my friend" Abraham Lincoln

True friendship carries a great deal of responsibility and is not a casual exercise. True friendship embraces quality interactions and a desire to seek each other's best interests. Viewing their relationships as true and dedicated friends, help to create an environment for new opportunities, support, and a working atmosphere in which individual differences are recognized. The results are usually visible, our daily greetings become meaningful, the other person's success becomes important to us, and their personal and professional problems become a little more important.

There will be a desire to coach and communicate frankly with their followers and mentor them to success. They want them to be successful and achieve greater success; *even if it puts them ahead of and above them.*

Leaders who consider the personal needs and beliefs of their members, have a much better chance of showing individual respect and worth. That in turn, directly creates commitment and a show of respect from the members.

Recognition is one of the most powerful tools available to a leader. Every man and or woman in the armed forces, industry, or business world, is unique and has an internal mechanism that craves attention and recognition. In nearly every job I have worked at, very few of my immediate supervisors knew much about me or my skills; other than what was within the scope of my job. Most employees are walking gold mines with talents and abilities that go untapped because leaders fail to get close to them.

Trust Is a Powerful Experience

When I was in the ninth grade, the principal of the school called my name over the intercom.

"Ed Shelton," he said, "could you please come to the office?"

Everyone looked at me as I nervously made my way out of the classroom, down the hall and into the principal's office. My mind was racing, as I tried to figure out what I might have done wrong. I couldn't think of anything, but I was sure that having the principal call you to his office was usually not a good sign.

The principal was not only the principal, but also the football coach. Mr. Freedman explained that he was going to hand out new play books to the team that afternoon.

"I need the books to hand out," he explained, "and I've left them in my apartment. Could you please go and get them for me?"

I sighed, a sigh of relief.

He then handed me the key to his apartment, and said, "This will let you in the front door. I left the books in my living room. When you leave, be sure to lock the door behind you."

Vicenza High School was an American school in Italy and had a dormitory next door where Mr. Freedman had a small apartment. I walked the short distance to his apartment; I held the key in my hand. It represented a great trust the principle had placed in me. He had chosen me as someone he could depend upon, that trust he placed in me felt good.

Building trust helps to build strong bonds between people, but we must earn that trust. Leaders must work to build it first, not the other way around.

My brother Ken was four years older than I was. He was my idol, I wanted to be just like him. I would follow him and his friends around and although I am sure he sometimes thought of me as a little pest, he was good to me and allowed me to tag along.

When Ken was in high school, he had saved enough money to buy himself a paper route. I remember well the day he came home and announced his new business venture. It was his pride and joy, and he spent many months saving the money to buy this route. One day as we were coming home, he stopped at the bus stop and asked me if I would like to help with the route. Of course

I would! I couldn't believe that he would trust me to pick up and deliver the papers – I knew how much it meant to him.

I arose, hours before school, and went down to the corner where I waited for the delivery of the papers. Other boys were there too waiting for the drop. I was the youngest, least experienced one there, but I recall how proud I was that my brother had trusted me. I worked hard to remain trusted, I made mistakes, but my brother never lost his trust in me. I was always grateful that he understood that there would be human errors and that it hadn't destroyed his trust in me.

Leaders must understand that trusting others means along with the opportunities come challenges. It is not only important to place trust in others, but it is important to know whom you can trust. You will learn many things and will need to make choices that will sometimes be difficult. You need to place your trust in those who will to do what is right. The biggest mistake you can ever make as a leader is to never trust anyone.

TRUST INDEX FOR LEADERS

_____ My supervisor keeps my interests in mind when making decisions.

_____ I would be willing to let my supervisor have complete control over my future in this company.

_____ If my supervisor asked why a problem occurred, I would speak freely even if I were partly to blame.

_____ I feel comfortable being creative because my supervisor understands that sometimes creative solutions do not work.

_____ It is important for me to have a good way to keep an eye on my supervisor.

_____ Increasing my vulnerability to criticism by my supervisor would be a mistake.

_____ If I had my way, I wouldn't let my supervisor have any influence over decisions that are important to me.

Response Scale

1	2	3	4	5
Strongly Disagree	Somewhat Disagree	Neither	Somewhat Agree	Strongly Agree

5

MOTIVATION

Leaders Motivate

The ability to motivate is a key element of leadership. Defining and under-standing motivation seems to be unclear for many mangers who usually know that it is important to achieve improved performance. Leaders who understand motivation, tend to first understand and possess four fundamental leadership qualities that include the following:

— **Intelligence**

— **Love of Learning**

— **Power of Introspection**

— **Respect for People**

Intelligence

First is the quality of intelligence. Intelligence is not just a matter of what IQ you are born with; intelligence can be increased through determined application and study. I have heard front-line managers say that they are not smart enough to lead or figure something out. They may come from home environments that reinforce this idea, and may tend to believe that no matter what happens, they have no control over how smart they are. The fact is, that intelligence is accumulated knowledge and can be added upon through reading, experiences, and observation. There is absolutely no need for anyone to go through their career resolved to not learn or grow. Leading others requires knowledge and learning.

Abraham Lincoln was a product of the backwoods of early America. He lost his mother at an early age and grew up with a father who belittled him and called him lazy. Through perseverance, he determined to self-educate himself and become a great lawyer and president.

Without opportunity for formal schooling, Abraham Lincoln was interested in almost every subject. He went from a backwoods nobody, to become a lawyer, state senator, and eventually President of the United States; all achieved without a formal education. He was a leader who achieved great things for the people and the country.

Eagerness to Learning

There is a second quality; a quality that you and I must have if we want to become effective leaders. It is a zeal for learning our trade or profession.

You may recall in the New Testament the story of a young student. He journeyed with his parents, Joseph and Mary, down to the feast of the Passover. We don't know why the party with whom he traveled to Jerusalem left before the feast was over, but it appears as if they did. They were some distance on their way, when Joseph and Mary discovered that their son was not with them. They went back and found him sitting at the feet—or standing before—some of the great Jewish teachers. At twelve years of age, Jesus Christ had a zeal for learning.

Benjamin Franklin, Abraham Lincoln, and all great public and business leaders I have met, are of like nature. Throughout their lives, a zeal for learning was one of their greatest qualities. There zeal became continuous with these leaders, never wavering.

Power of Introspection

Most great leaders have another quality that is important to all of us. It is the power of introspection—the power to look within ourselves and see what kind of person we are.

Every morning, each one of us looks into a mirror to examine our physical appearance—hair styling, makeup, general health. Have you ever thought how fine it would be to look within yourself—to meet yourself on the street and ask yourself what kind of a person you are, to interrogate yourself? Do you know your own faults, your own strengths?

Here is an interesting quality of most leaders who trust and are trusted. They know their own weaknesses and strengths, and they work to develop their weaknesses into strengths.

Most of us hide our weaknesses. In the business world, I have witnessed many, good managers and workers destined for failure, due to fully following the directions and instructions, given them by their boss. It is at these moments, lesser leaders do not acknowledge their errors, and try to hide their weaknesses or failures. Effective leaders accept the reprimands, acknowledge and correct the errors, building greater trust in the process.

As leaders, it is important and okay to recognize that we have many weaknesses, but we must set about to overcome them.

Respect for People

Let me refer to another characteristic of an effective leader which has been a key theme in this book; *respect for people*.

No leader can be great in this world without a deep respect for those who work for them.

The challenge for the leader in any organization is to engage in the kinds of actions that will let those who work with or under him, know that he has a vital, personal concern about them as individuals.

Dr. Rensis Likert, formerly of the University of Michigan, has stated that a fundamental condition of an effective organization is the degree to which it conforms to what he calls the "principle of supportive relationships."

This principle is defined as follows:

"The leadership and other processes of the organization must be such as to ensure a maximum probability that in all interactions and in all relationships within the organization, each member, in the light of his background, values, desires, and expectations, will view the experience as supportive and one which builds and maintains his sense of personal worth and importance."

No organization can exist for long unless work is completed, and goals are accomplished. The leader cannot ignore work-centered activities, and he should see that activities are planned, programs are set up, materials are in order, and assignments are made and followed through. But all of this must be done in the general atmosphere of an overriding concern for those who must do the work and carry out the assignments. When people feel like their superiors think the work is more important than the people who do it, motivation to work is hindered.

This is the critical balance—good planning, organization, and high performance standards for work, in an atmosphere where each individual involved feels confident that he, personally, is understood, appreciated, and highly involved.

What can be done by leaders to create an atmosphere of personal concern and individual acceptance?

Four Principles on Becoming a Leader of Genuine Concern

1. Take time

Too often the interaction at work is hurried, poorly timed, and conducted with the feeling, "We're both busy, so let's hurry and get this over with." Find little bits of time regularly, for quick expressions of appreciation, an interview, or an oral evaluation. These should be scheduled with time enough to express real appreciation, to find out any personal concerns, and to talk about, not only the job, but also the person.

2. Ask personal questions

For many reasons, leaders shy away from talking personally with others. It seems safer to talk business. But one can move into the area of personal concern by saying something like the following: "I honestly would like to know how you feel about your work, and if it conflicts with your family. If you have any qualms or reservations, I would like to know; and if you have any suggestions for improving things, they would be most welcome," or "How are things going for you now? Are you having any problems, questions, or difficulties with which I can help?"

It may be possible to open up a discussion of something you, the leader, have noticed is bothering the other person.

3. Listen with understanding.

If a person begins to talk about feelings of concern about matters that affect him, the leader must listen, and listen, and listen; then try to understand. It will not be helpful if the leader invites sharing and then interrupts with such comments as, "That's not how it really is,"; "You didn't really get a clear picture of what we are trying to do,"; "Let me tell you what I would do if I was you," or "That's not the way we do things here."

They can listen with understanding or empathy. This means honestly trying to see the problem or the situation from the other person's position, and to try to understand how and why he sees and responds to things the way he does. This way, help can be given from where *he* is rather than from where the *leader* is.

4. Be willing to do something.

One of the most common reactions of the leader after a person has shared a real concern is to ask, "How can I help?"

This question often puts the person being interviewed in a real dilemma. He may not have been asking for help, and he may not know what would be the appropriate thing to say.

Feeling awkward and embarrassed he may say, "Oh, I don't need any help," or "I don't know what you could do."

Instead of asking what he can do, the leader can actually do something; he can take action. He can express understanding, concern, and empathy and respond with an expression of support or gratitude, a touch or a pat on the back.

He can suggest action, such as: "I know that this project is difficult; let me go to the production line this week see it for myself." "That's a tough problem. Let me talk to the president and get his reaction."

If one has real concern, he can usually do something that reflects through his actions that his concern is real, and not just a ploy used because he has read an article on personal concern and feels he ought to try it.

Do your workers behave the way you expect them to behave? Is their behavior based upon your attitude toward them? Is honest praise a good motivational and directional force?

Self-Fulfilling Prophecy

Research suggests that the answer is yes. Your attitude as a leader creates the environment in which your workers exist. A leader becomes an environmental creator. For example, quite unconsciously, leaders interact with their workers so that they may receive the response they expect to receive.

Several years ago, I was part of a study that examined leadership preference of over one hundred immigrant workers, and over one hundred non-immigrant workers at a meat processing plant. At random, five percent of the workers from each department were selected as an experimental group. Their managers were told that these particular workers had scored high on the leadership test and would show remarkable gains in leadership development during the next few months. Actually, the only difference between these workers and the others in the plant was in the minds of the production managers.

By the end of six months, the workers designated as "talented", had received higher performance reviews than did the other workers in the other group. The department managers and supervisors were asked to describe the work behavior of their "talented" workers. They were seen as harder working, more detailed, and responsive.

Studies of this nature demonstrate the widespread tendency of people to behave the way others expect them to behave; a pattern known as the self-fulfilling prophecy. If we really believe that people will behave in a certain way, then our attitude is based on that expectation. In turn, our attitude produces the expected behavior.

If you continually tell a child he is lazy and no good, you will have a lazy no good child. If you tell a worker that things are not working out, things will not work out. Self-fulfilling prophecy applied in negative terms can kill the workforce.

As a leader I decided early in my career that I would not use casual phrases that undermine, degrade others or suggest failure to others. If it was not uplifting and positive, I would leave the issue alone.

Literature and research, suggest that positive feedback, honest praise, and recognition for work well done, reinforce self-motivation and make people feel good. Negative reactions and the assignments of tasks beyond one's abilities, can break down both a person's self-motivation and his self-esteem.

This cycle develops into a vicious circle, where a manager or supervisor perceiving a worker is a poor performer, lazy or does not care, treats the worker accordingly; and the worker will respond accordingly. This response reinforces the manager's attitude and a completely negative relationship ensues.

If leaders seek and exploit the workers better qualities, and act as though the worker is a valuable part of the team offering honest praise for work well done, then the worker will most likely react favorably and a positive relationship exists.

Responsibility for improving leadership skills is the responsibility of the manager or leader themselves and those appointed over them. However, it is the leader who is the only one, in the last analysis, who can break the self fulfilling cycle.

I learned firsthand the power and beauty of this principle while serving as a Human Resources Director in North Carolina. The president of Human Resources was coming to visit for the first time. I was somewhat anxious about this first visit, since I didn't know him very well personally. I was relatively young and inexperienced, and didn't want anything to undermine the confidence placed in me. Frankly, I was somewhat guarded and apprehensive.

However, from our first meeting, the president's attitude was, "What are you trying to accomplish and how can I help you?"

His sincerity totally disarmed me. I felt he was there to help me, not to judge me. I therefore freely shared our problems and goals and asked for his help. I had available the invaluable resources of a very experienced, wise, and effective leader.

During his visit, I invited him to join me and my staff of 12 for a meeting to discuss some important union issues. I remember that during the meeting, some of the staff began voicing concerns and looked to our guest for sympathy.

He answered, in substance, "These, of course, are for Ed's attention. I'm here to sustain and help him. He will have to deal with these concerns that you have expressed."

What would have happened if he had been openly sympathetic with some of their views? Where would they have looked for leadership? Not to him, for he was returning to Virginia, and had many HR divisions to supervise. He couldn't possibly get involved on a regular basis in details of local affairs.

Instead, I felt sustained. How responsible I felt! How committed! How motivated to make things work! How open I was to his advice and ideas and help! If I had doubts or questions about the sincere concerns raised, I would privately ask him.

His basic answer was, "You might consider what they're doing in this or that issue." This left me with the decision and the responsibility.

Those who have worked with hovering supervisors know how it undermines one's sense of responsibility and initiative. You simply can't delegate responsibility for results and supervise methods very closely. If you do, you take back the responsibility.

It is far better to teach correct management principles, and let those under you make decisions themselves in light of those principles. Then you have built all your judgments into those principles and you become their helper, their leader. Even if they falter or fail altogether, you always return to discuss the original assignment or agreement, and either revise it or renew it together.

Critical to ensuring that people are allowed to act and make decisions, is the leaders' willingness to self-examine oneself. Self-examination is most difficult. Surveys have shown that most people take credit for success but blame their failures on external forces or other people. It would be well, when confronted with a problem, to be able to ask – is the problem me?

Leadership requires the application of self-examination, and to have the courage, fortitude, and wisdom to apply self-examination. Or will you, as many do, be inclined to try and decide which of your associates will fail.

Dale Carnegie once said, "If you are not in the process of becoming the person you want to be, you are automatically engaged in becoming the person you don't want to be."

Committed leaders will not permit those under them to engage in destructive criticism, retaliation, or undue disgust. We should commit ourselves to marching, shoulder to shoulder, with our workers—without destroying, condemning, or belittling.

I'm thinking of an employee at a plant in Jackson, Ohio, where I served on the management team. The employee fell off a platform he was working from.

To my question, "Why did you fall off the platform?" he replied, "I fell out because I wasn't in far enough!"

It has been my experience over the years that, generally speaking, those employees who fall "out" of the workforce, were never "in" far enough. The leaders have failed to insure that the employee's best interests were met, and they never felt they were accepted as part of the team. They have not been made a part of the social system.

In a simple statement, the difference between those leaders who are committed and those who are not, is the difference between the words *want* and *will*.

For example, "I want to be a effective leader, but the employees are too lazy or hard to work with," or "I will be effective and make sure I create the proper environment and provide the proper tools for them to be successful." "I would like to be a good leader, but look what I have to work with" or "I will be an effective and good leader."

Effective Leaders do not Motivate by Fear or Discipline

A leader who depends on reward systems, regulations, policy, position and the power of disciplinary action to motivate and carry out assignments, simply does not understand what motivation is. Known in the academic circles as transactional or implicit contracting leadership, this is the most commonly applied leadership style and the least effective. It is what separates effective leaders from average and ineffective leaders. It creates a relationship based on explicit contracts or a *quid pro qua* (…I will give you this in exchange for that) relationship. It is conditional, and tends to defocus on the individual and more on the system.

Many leaders fail because of power-dominance; having a real or perceived need to dominate those under them. Triggered by attitudes or learned behavior, domination is a self-centered attribute that drives leaders to seek their own interests over their follower's. The problem is that most followers easily and quickly recognize domination as being self-centered, and resist either passively or openly.

The HMS Bounty

No story can better illustrate failed leadership than that of the HMS Bounty. Several movies have been made, but perhaps the best made was with Marlin Brando, who played Mr. Christianson.

In the movie, Mutiny on the Bounty, Captain Bligh is the new Captain of the HMS Bounty. He has been appointed by the Royal Court to sail to the South pacific in search for breadfruit. Shortly after departing England, the Captain is confronted by the ships logistical officer, who reports that there is some cheese missing. Capt. Bligh orders the rations to be cut until the shortage is made up.

As Captain Bligh and Mr. Christian are going down below, they overhear a sailor accusing Capt. Bligh of stealing the cheese. Confronting the sailor, he asks Mr. Christianson what he recommends, to which Mr. Christianson suggests two weeks without grog. Capt. Bligh orders the man to be punished with twenty-four lashes in front of the crew.

On deck, the punishment is about to begin, when the designated, whipping sailor leans over and whispers to the accused, "Remember it's not me", to which the sailor replies, "It's okay, I can take it".

The lashing begins and by the twelfth lash, all are becoming squeamish and visibly disturbed with the brutality of the punishment. The sailor is taken down and the crew dismissed.

That evening at Officer Mess, Captain Bligh sees that the officers appetites are wanting and asks Mr. Christianson what the problem is and to speak freely. Mr., Christian tells Bligh that he felt the punishment was too severe. Capt. Bligh then gives a lecture to the officers:

"You will all be Captains in charge of your own ship one day. Let me describe the typical seaman. He is half-witted, a wife-beater, a habitual drunkard, and he spends his whole life evading and defying authority. What makes this man go aloft? I tell you, it's fear. Now, I'm not a man for cruelty or barbarism, but cruelty with purpose is not cruelty, its efficiency. A man will never disobey you when once he's seen his mate's backbone laid bare, he'll remember those white ribs staring at him; he'll see the flesh jump, hear the whistle of the whip for the rest of his life."

Mr Christian ponders this lecture for several minutes then proclaims, "Perhaps you are right. (There is a long pause as Captain Bligh picks up a sliver of cheese). I would be careful with that cheese if I were you sir, it has a peculiar smell. I believe it's a bit tainted. But of course, it's a matter if individual taste."

In a diplomatic way, Mr. Christiansen has pointed out that he does not agree with Bligh's style of leadership. This particular episode describes many leaders who believe in "motivation by fear". While Bligh may seem extreme, I would argue that in today's organizations, it is more common than one would think. While conducting leadership training, I am often taken back by how many bosses come to me and express their belief in fear-based leadership.

Several years ago, I worked for one of the finest plant mangers I have ever known. Ray Parma and I were developing several new initiatives to improve communications between management and the employees. We began with employee assessments, 360 feedback, and open lunch forums between the employees and Ray, the plant manager. The sessions were so successful that the plant was designated the top performing plant in the nation out of a field of over twenty-eight others.

Early in the program, we made a decision to take the employee comments to the supervisor meetings where the issue would be discussed, and in many cases, hold supervisors accountable. During one meeting with the supervisors, a comment was made, "we are being too soft on the employees, what's wrong with putting fear into them?"

Basically the supervisor was saying, "It's too hard to manage with effective communications and accountability, it's easier to mange with fear."

The fact is he was correct. Leading by fear is very easy and does not take much effort other than a little ranting, raging and threatening.

In a brilliant, thoughtful response, Ray Parma, with his typically patient manner, thought for a few seconds then looked at the supervisor and said,

"Okay, I will go along with that idea, but first let me make sure that we set the example here. I plan to severely reprimand, perhaps even terminate, the next supervisor whose department falls below the expected P&L goals."

There was dead silence. The point had been made. No one wants to be led by fear.

Case in History – Leading Through Fear

It has been speculated that under Stalin's leadership, more people were put to death for political and cultural reasons than during Hitler's invasion. Stalin's methods were fear-based. He believed that fear was necessary in order to accomplish his vision of Russia's future. Under his orders during WW II, he ordered the organization of the NKVD, a Para-military group that searched the war zones and adjacent areas for deserters or malingerers, and summarily execute them. His reign of terror began in 1936 and ended at his death in 1939. Stalin's leadership led to over two million, soviet citizens being placed in concentration camp Gulag's, where they would die of starvation, forced labor, and exposure from the harsh Siberian winters.

Nikita Khrushchev's "Secret Speech"

In 1956, Nikita Khrushchev delivered a blistering speech about the tyranny of Joseph Stalin. The speech broke Stalin's spell, by telling the truth about his crimes and began the process that abolished the Soviet Union thirty years later. In Nikita Khrushchev's 1956 speech, he addressed the soviet political elites with a off-the record speech that renounced Stalin and his dogma. It was a denunciation of Stalin and his actions against the Soviet people. The speech shocked many of the communist hard liners in attendance. Then, somewhere in the crowd, came a pointed question from one of the younger communist members.

"If you knew what was going on, why didn't you do something?"

Nikita glared out at the audience and, slamming his closed fist onto the podium he demanded, "Who said that?"

Silence… not a man spoke.

He demanded again, slamming his fist on the podium harder, "Tell me, who said that."

Again, not a stir, no one dared stand up or say a word.

Khrushchev yelled into the microphone, pointing his finger at the assembly, "I want to know, who said that, now!"

The silence was penetrating.

After several minutes, he leaned forward and in a firm, audible whisper he said, "That's why we did nothing."

The point was made clear; these strong willed Soviet leaders were brought to their knees because of fear.

The problem with leading by fear is that it is temporary and cannot be sustained; it requires perpetuating the fear factor, which in turn causes resentment and loss of trust and respect from the followers. It is similar to a brutish father who uses capitol punishment on his children; they will immediately obey today, but tomorrow they will despise and resent his brutality.

To help better understand this concept of leading by fear and the negative aspects that it brings to people and relationships, I have developed the following comparison for you to review. You will see that those qualities under the Tyrannical Leader are undesirable and can not be uplifting or positive. So why do leaders in today's workplace feel fear is appropriate?

PROFILE OF A MOTIVATIONAL LEADER:

Leaders That Motivate	Leaders That De-motivate
Generous with his time and talents	Holds back his praise and recognition
Erases all economical and social barriers	Holds those less fortunate in contempt
Focuses on others growth	Self-centered
Uplifts and encourages	Condemns and intimidates
Is trusted, respected and approachable	Is feared and avoided
Level-headed and calm	Easily agitated, flies off into rages
Exposes others to opportunities	Condemns and insults others in public

Reviewing historical leaders such as Hitler, Custer, Stalin and some bosses you may have worked for, the question is, why did they use fear? The answer may be that they saw fear as leadership strength, and in every case, nothing they achieved was helpful to the organization or its leadership. Not one of them was trusted or respected by their followers. They did okay in getting results but never were able to go beyond that. Their followers gave no extra effort and denied the organization of their creative knowledge and energy. Let me list for you what fear does to a group:

- People tend to focus on basic issues, neglecting more complicated tasks
- People are not willing to take risks.
- Creative energy is misdirected.
- People are satisfied with achieving short term results.
- Organizational goals and wellbeing are abandoned for personal security.
- Flexible ideas and policies transform into rigid policies.
- Communication tends to be filtered up. No one wants to talk to the boss, and when communications happens, it's calculated and risk-free.
- It creates bonding within small chat groups; none of which help to build the organization or add value for the leader.

Why are leaders attracted to leading by fear? Perhaps the philosophy of feared leaders rational can best be described in his manual, The Prince, Machiavelli.

"One ought to be both feared and loved, but as it is difficult for the two to go together, it is much safer to be feared than loved… for love is held by a chain of obligation which, men being selfish, is broken whenever it serves their purpose; but fear is maintained by a dread of punishment which never fails."

The Prince, Niccolo Machiavelli:

Using Disciplinary Actions

Another use of fear is that of using discipline within a group or team setting. Using discipline may be necessary at times but it must be used in good judgement and is a leadership call. There has to be consequences for actions and discipline, but too much, or unnecessary discipline can demoralize people or the group very quickly.

Over the years, I have adopted what I have termed the "Physicians Rule" in disciplining people. It came to me one afternoon as a supervisor was sitting in front of me, trying to convince me that an employee who had caused some product damage should be fired. The employee had been with the company for fifteen years, and had a dedicated service record. However, new policies enacted required immediate termination for damages by employees over certain set dollar amount. The problem I saw was that we were about to let go of fifteen years of institutional knowledge, destroy a social network, and cause unnecessary job security concerns among the other workers. As I sat there, my mind raced back to when I was sixteen.

When I was sixteen, I was involved in a particularly gruesome accident to my hand. In the emergency room, I was given medication to relieve my pain and was going in and out of consciousness. I recall a young medical doctor coming to my side and telling me that they could not save my hand, it would have to be partially amputated. I was in no position to answer or respond. I just looked up into the face of the young doctor. His decision would have to be final. As the medical team gathered around, I could see the different devices used for the procedure. A nurse stood over me and told me that I would not feel much pain, but there would be a slight burning sensation. Just as she said that, an older, more experienced doctor came in and stood by my side.

I recall him saying, "This is too radical, let me do something different, it will be better for him long term."

I'm not sure what he meant or what he did, but I know today I am better off for his wisdom and experience. I am missing a portion of my finger, but I have had the benefit of my hand since that time.

Coming back to the employee waiting disciplinary action, I told the supervisor, "Let's use the least radical surgery to cure this problem."

Another solution was taken, the employee was held accountable, his talents preserved, and his sense of fairness supported. Everyone came away better off.

Use the least radical surgery to cure the problem.

POINTS OF DISCUSSION

Why did Nikita Khrushchev give his "secret speech"?

What points was he trying to make to the politicians?

How can it apply to business and your organization?

What did Captain Bligh mean when he said "cruelty with purpose is not cruelty, its efficiency," and how does that apply today? Do leaders use cruelty to gain efficiency?

6

PERSONALITY DISORDERS AND LEADERSHIP

"Nearly all men can stand adversity, but if you want to test a man's character, give him power." Abraham Lincoln

At every speaking engagement on leadership, I am always asked the ultimate question.

"What are the main causes of ineffective leadership?"

While the answer is not simple nor can it be focused on one single element, most of it can be traced to selfishness and self interests. Then it becomes even more complicated, because the definition of "ineffective" varies to a great degree.

In order to give a good understanding of ineffective, you must understand that often times, a leader with charismatic style who is popular within the top members of the organization, is usually, in reality a paradoxical hero; a person both loved and hated, idealized and scorned, a person not crazy, but thought to be by some of his followers. The leader usually display's a complex character and personality that is confusing and misdirected at times. This complexity of personality may be driven by unresolved struggles within the leader, and is what makes them volatile and ineffective. The ineffectiveness can be measured by six simple factors;

1. Making decisions independent of the group.
2. Show anger when challenged.
3. People are quickly fired or leave (high turnover).
4. Fails to tap into ideas and talents of the group.
5. Covers up bad decisions by blaming others.
6. Gets results, but damages other's integrity and enthusiasm.

Ineffective leaders may have many successes, but eventually the damage created underneath the radar is revealed over time or through a catastrophic event. The best way to understand how this develops is to better understand the individual personalities of these ineffective leaders.

Individual personality inevitably causes one to encounter the essential character of that person, and their unique and individual identities. Often, people are said to have either strong or outgoing personalities based on behavior patterns they exhibit that are distinctive and consistent. Leaders may be described in terms such as, "driven", "intense", "direct", "focused" or "no-nonsense"… all terms which refer to some characteristic of that leader's personality.

For most leaders, these characteristics, as described by those around them, do not usually affect the group unless that characteristic is both persistent over time and across situations. For example, if your boss loses his temper one time in a year, that is not automatically a characteristic of that boss. But if the boss looses his temper every time his authority is challenged, that becomes a characteristic trait or "quirk," that can often times, be very destructive to the group and individuals. It is these personality characteristics, or "personality disorders," that make a leader ineffective.

Personality disorders are defined as, inflexible and enduring patterns of behavior that impair in some way, a leader's group functioning and limit maximum effectiveness. The disorders that the leader faces, becomes damaging or maladaptive if the leader is unable to modify the behavior when the situation or issue undergoes significant change calling for a different approach. The leader either cannot, or is not willing to adapt his or her behavior. Most leaders have only one or two characteristics of disorder, which do not significantly impair functioning as does a full-blown disorder. Only when personality becomes inflexible and maladaptive and causes significant function impairment or follower distress, does it become a personality disorder. The most common disorder for most leaders and bosses is a behavior disorder called **narcissism**.

The roots of the term "narcissism," originate from the classic Greek tragedy written by the Roman poet, Ovid Narcissus. It is the story of a spoiled, beautiful, young man named Narcissus, who found himself loved by several maidens and would-be suitors through the forests of his homeland. As the son of the nymph Leriope, and the river-god Ceohissus, it is prophesized by the seer Tiresias, that Narcissus would live to a ripe old age, provided that he never knew himself. A stubborn and prideful boy, Narcissus rejected all who would desire his love and attention. Among those he rejected was the nymph Echo, who fell in love with Narcissus, but Narcissus cruelly rejected her. The nymphs prayed that Narcissus might love and feel the pains of rejection and not gain the thing that he loved. The prayer was heard and Narcissus was confronted with and then fell in love with, his own reflection while walking in the gardens of Echo. Narcissus embraced the loved reflection, but it fled at his touch and returned again to fascinate him. His image apparently welcomed him; when he approached it, it approached him; when he stretched out his arms to it, it stretched out its arms to him. It seemed to want to be embraced, yet it fled when touched. As the tragedy unfolds, Narcissus grieves for the image that he could see but not embrace ultimately realizing his passion was for the image of himself. Falling deeply in love with himself, he slowly wasted his days in awe of his reflection. After lying on the bank admiring his reflection, he became incapable of loving others. As potential lovers approached him, seeking his attention and love, he quietly turned away and eventually died.

Narcissism derives its name from Narcissus, and both derive from the Greek word *narke* "numb" from which we also get the word narcotic. Thus for the Greeks, Narcissus stood for vanity, callousness and insensitivity, as he was emotionally numb to the entreaties of those who fell in love with his beauty.

Today, we can see leaders with narcissism as being selfish, those who desire their own best interests, and not those of whom they serve. It is the root of most ineffective leadership, and being a behavior, can only be reformed by the leader themselves. This concept is particularly applicable to the relationship between those who, for example, become successful people in their own business, in the corporation, politics or other segments of society. In a sense, the narcissistic leader's view of themselves is justified by the views of others they surround themselves with.

Among top organizational leaders and politicians, there is a degree of narcissism which may be considered an asset, especially among those who are "self-made," or who owe their success to those above them. The leader tends to regulate their own self-esteem through the manipulation of those under him or her. This is often manifested through conditioning of the group with anger, fear, reward and punishment, and even to the point of getting rid of those who do not acknowledge the leaders power and control, or who challenge the leader's authority.

The narcissistic leader develops cracks in his or her effectiveness caused by the need for grandiosity. Grandiosity is observed by others as a pattern of self-importance, expectations of being recognized, preoccupation with fantasies of unlimited success or power, and a belief in one's uniqueness and sense of entitlement. Clear examples surface every day, cases such as Col. Oliver North, who during the Contra Iran scandal, embezzled money orders and accepted unauthorized gifts in the form of a security system for his home. Ken Lay of Enron, who was convicted on charges of corruption and abuse of power. Thomas Coughlin, and the former head of Wal-Mart's US retail operations was forced to resign from the board, after allegations that up to $500,000 was obtained from the company through unauthorised use of gift cards and false expense reports. The list goes on, and will continue to grow as leaders get caught up in the network of power and sense of entitlement; a classical symptom of narcissism and selfishness.

Grandiosity – "I am better than you."

Grandiosity is a symptom of bad leadership, it is the attitude that I am better than you and can cripple a leader when he or she really begins to believe there ultimate superiority. There are eight components of grandiosity found in leaders with personality quirks associated with narcissism:

1. The leader exaggerates talents, capacity, and achievements in an unrealistic way.

2. The leader believes in their own invulnerability or do not recognize their limitations.

3. The leader believes they do not need other people.

4. The person regards themselves as unique or special compared to others.

5. The leader regards themselves as generally superior to others.

6. The leader becomes self-centered; disregarding other's ideas and opinions.

7. The leader appears or behaves in a boastful way.

8. The leader is arrogant and haughty. They are viewed as snobbish, better than others, and patronizing towards others.

Many leaders who are vulnerable to narcissism also have tendencies to go into unreasonable rages, followed by embarrassment and shame, having very little control at stopping or limiting them. These rages are often triggered or occur in response to perceived slights, rebuffs, and rejections, and thus, are clearly related to their need for control and power. The leader views him or her, as being attacked, and tends to take issues personal. This may be a response to defend their status and position of power. When in actuality, the perceived attacks are simply a healthy exchange of opinions and ideas that, under normal leadership, is encouraged and supported.

I have witnessed narcissistic leaders go into an emotional stage similar to pouting, visibly withdrawing their emotional support, stopping meaningful engagement, and essentially shutting others out. It is the grandiose qualities of the leader that under normal circumstances, suffice to protect the ego of these leaders. But when internal experiences become more than the person's protective barriers can handle, the result is usually an almost uncontrollable rage/child-like cycle. I have also noticed that in these leaders, there is a correlation between education and the intensity of the cycle. Most leaders who fall into these rages may be limited in education, lack the ability to understand or develop protective barriers, and lack an understanding of how their behaviour impacts others.

How Did They Get In Position of Leadership?

Most managers and leaders you know in your organization have been promoted because they demonstrated ambition and were able to control or manage small volumes of processes or people. As those managers move up into the organization they are given more power and authority. As a result, personalities can be transformed and style changed, as their egos are fed by power. As people climb higher up this power structure, more time is spent by the leader on his or her ego functions and less on the needs of the organization and others. So it's not surprising when you hear the phrase, "power corrupts"; it may be true. It becomes devastating to the organization and those who work for leaders who become caught up in the power cycle and fail to control their narcissistic tendencies.

It is important to realize that we all have narcissistic tendencies, but it is a matter of recognizing and controlling them and not letting them create an unhealthy management style.

Seven Signs of Narcissistic Leaders

1. Overly concerned with "how they look".
2. Rigid.
3. Preoccupied with details.
4. Demonstrates an unusual need for control.
5. Demonstrates an excessive devotion to work and productivity.
6. Does not trust others and lacks empathy.
7. Lacks the ability to develop personal relationships.

One of the problems with narcissism is that it creates a paranoia behavior, making it difficult for these managers and leaders to be accessible to their employees, because they tend to loose trust in everyone except a small hand-picked group of associates. It is usually disguised by being too busy with a full schedule that does not allow time for reflecting and evaluating. They spend time micro-managing and controlling every process.

Self-centeredness, distrust of their employees, and their need for absolute control, cause these leaders to be perceived as superficial and fake, and in turn the leaders develop a suspicious view of their workers. They focus too much on the outward person; their problems, mistakes, and faults, failing to recognize their individual talents and potential. Narcissistic leaders tend to surround themselves with managers and leaders who have the similar quality of exploiting others, and who will support their views and opinions even when they know their advice and views are wrong.

The tragedy of narcissist leaders is that over time, a culture within the group or organization begins to emerge characterized by mistrust; change is controlled, spontaneous ideas and creativity are discouraged. The top becomes filled with "yes" men, who limit their contribution to what the leader wants to hear by filtering information up to the top. Another damaging effect to the followers and organization is the emotional toll it takes on the team, as their personal values are ignored or in some cases attacked. Employees become neglected when there is no recognition, reward, or meaningful communication. Employees become less committed, hostile towards the organization and eventually find other work. Teams can not survive since there is no support for the manager or his ideas. Most effective leaders realize that building trust requires them to positively drive their people's moods and performance. They understand that fear and anger are a mobilizing force; but is very short term. Narcissist leaders fail to comprehend these principles as an aid for motivation and team building. They fail to mobilize the talents and commitment of the people.

The most concerning and dangerous characteristic of narcissistic leaders, is that they seldom give up power; they may delegate simple tasks, but never the power. They will impose strict rules and guidelines; impose fuzzy boundaries where cohesion is impossible to attain. They refuse responsibility; they are the declared experts, making others feel inferior and guilty. Every failure is criticized and announced so that a fear develops for failure. It is in these organizations that lying and falsification of numbers and information occurs, because of the perceived reprisals.

One of their problems that narcissistic leaders universally demonstrated is that they are highly manipulative. Their actions and motives do not spring from a deep sense of caring for others, but from a need to use them to achieve their own goals and satisfy their own needs. These leaders are not focused on the long term affect of their actions, but rush to solve problems by seeking to stop the present pain, and thereby create greater difficulty and pain later on.

Do not confuse Narcissism with Quirkiness or Ambition

Narcissism can be confused with quirks, which are magnified character traits. Quirks usually do not have the same long term impact that narcissist leaders have on others. Quirks are magnified behavior preferences, such as a boss who demands a clean desk as a sign of organization, or a boss who becomes irritated when people are late for a meeting; neither have an impact on the bottom line or on the organization, it is simply irritating to the leader. A quirk becomes a disorder when it impacts the talent pool or the ability of the organization to function. Quirkiness is a prelude to Narcissism but is not as serious and often does not distract from the leader's effectiveness.

Ambition unlike quirkiness is not a bad trait, and may be absolutely necessary for effective leadership. Ambition is best described as energy and determination, good when balanced and dangerous unbalanced. People without energy are those who say, "One day I will be in a better position," but then, never get there. It is critical for leaders to have the ability to stay focused and on task, through completion. Finally, if you want to determine if your ambition is unbalanced, ask yourself this question. Am I driven to succeed at the expense of others, or am I driven to succeed collectively, that all may benefit? Ambition directed toward the benefit of others is an important quality for us all to obtain.

As an undergraduate student years ago, I heard a speaker talk about ambition and how important education was to each of us who were graduating. The speaker stated that the more education we could obtain, the more the world would reward us.

He then followed the comment by saying, "But after all the worldly rewards, I would suggest to you that the real purpose of your education is to help others and better their lives the best that you can."

Ambition with direction and purpose is essential for effective and purposeful leadership. Better stated; "ambition with benevolence is an ideal leadership characteristic.

Why It's Important to Understand Personality Disorders

The importance of why personality disorders occur in leaders is essential for us to understand, because of the influence of character on organizations and the people who are influenced by them. If we know that healthy leaders can profoundly have positive influence of organizational results and people, then unhealthy leadership has an equal impact and affects with negative impact and influence. Leaders have impact upon the employees and for this reason, the character and behavior of a leader should be of interest to the organizational leaders. Logic would suggest that the pathology of the organization is a result of the pathology of its leaders.

A certain amount of ego and narcissism are necessary, and may be needed to function as a leader; however, the stronger the narcissist tendency, the more vulnerable the leader becomes to over stimulation as result of power and sense to protect self. These leaders develop the need for power and prestige, and assume positions of authority and leadership. Individuals with such characteristics are found rather frequently in top leadership positions. It is the responsibility of investors and top leaders, to insure that these leaders' motives are understood and that those who are motivated for power and prestige are prevented from reaching the bowels of the organization.

Labeling bad bosses as having personality disorders is not fair or always accurate but the fact is there are some bosses/leaders, which are a pleasure to work for. They are kind, helpful, honest, benevolent, and motivating. Then there are those who are abrupt, blunt, direct, intense, and cold-hearted. They lack the ability to motivate and inspire. We avoid them, minimize communications with them and most of all do not enjoy being around them. The first type boss arouses in us an eagerness to participate, engage and be at work. The other boss creates in us a fear, avoidance, even hostility.

EXERCISE

What reaction do you instill in those under you? Take this quiz to help you determine your style.

- People consider you hard to approach and may avoid talking with you.

- Too busy to greet people and say hi.

- You dominate meetings with your comments.

- Are quick to attack and may lose your temper.

- Use the word "I" a lot in your conversation.

- You avoid taking responsibility and find blame in others.

- You are afraid to lose position or power.

- You are more critical than not. You use terms such as "I don't care – fix it", "no excuses", "if they can't do the job, get rid of them" or "getting them on the ball", "They just weren't working out."

7

COURAGE

Character is More Important than Skills and Knowledge

The decisions we make as leaders and the way we behave are what ultimately shape our character. Charles A. Hall aptly described that process in these lines:

"We sow our thoughts, and we reap our actions; we sow our actions, and we reap our habits; we sow our habits, and we reap our characters; we sow our characters, and we reap our destiny"

Courage; it is an absolute for leaders. In fact, I would suggest that without courage, you cannot be an effective leader at home, the workplace, or in society in general. It is the fabric that good leaders are cut from and allows for bold decisions and acts. There are two types of courage that are essential for effective leadership.

Can courage be learned? It can, in the sense that the development of deep devotion to a cause galvanizes a person to act on behalf of that cause. This type of fundamental belief in the value of the mission is essential to the cultivation of courage, whether it be physical or moral.

Only a profound conviction that there is a good greater than self can spark a person to risk everything for others. Self-sacrifice, and the courage to take that chance, is the antithesis of a "me-generation" philosophy. When the lives or liberties of others are valued more highly than one's own life, then true courage can provide the fuel for remarkable accomplishments.

Two Faces of Courage – Physical and Moral

Leaders must understand what courage is. There are different kinds of courage – physical courage and moral courage.

First let me discuss physical courage. When a sense of mission becomes powerful enough to motivate people to action, even in the face of personal danger or certain death that is physical courage. To be courageous one need not be fearless; it is natural and good to be afraid when confronted with real risks. But so long as that fear does not paralyze, there is courage at work.

Raoul Wallenberg's story demonstrates physical courage, as he ignored armed soldiers and even flying bullets to continue his rescue operations. He had the audacity to threaten high-ranking Nazi officers, who had proved their willingness to murder innocent civilians, let alone troublesome opponents, under conditions where they easily could have killed him. Although in constant fear for his life, he pressed on, risking and ultimately sacrificing himself for his mission.

The second is moral courage, which is defined by one's unwavering belief and values of right and wrong and as defined by personal commitment. It is my experience however, that leaders with moral courage, (that is, one who is true to himself), also have physical courage. In William Shakespeare's play, Hamlet, the character Polonius, instructs his son on many aspects of his conduct. And he concludes a rather long statement with these words: **"To thine own self be true."**

THE RAOUL WALLENBERG STORY OF COURAGE

No story better illustrates courage than Raoul Wallenberg. The story is best told by an excerpt from, The Journal of Leadership Studies, 1997, Vol. 4, No. 3, authored by John Kunich and Richard Lestaer.

Raoul Wallenberg was a Swedish diplomat who went to Budapest in 1944 to intervene on behalf of Hungary's 700,000 Jews, who were being deported by the Nazis to extermination camps.

During the waning months of World War II, the Allies were desperate for ways to stop Hitler's slaughter of innocent civilians in Eastern Europe. Even as the prospects for an Axis military victory dimmed, the Nazis grew more determined to complete the "final solution." Death camps operated at maximum capacity in a feverish effort to rid Europe of Jews, and other target groups. Until a complete military triumph could be secured, the Allies were powerless to halt the genocide raging on behind enemy lines. Therefore, a volunteer was sought--someone who could go where allied tanks and aircraft could not, and disrupt the insidious, Nazi death machine.

No one could have been a less obvious choice for this mission than Raoul Wallenberg. Wallenberg was 32 years old in 1944, a wealthy, upper-class Swede from a prominent, well-respected family. Sweden's neutrality in the war was only one in a long series of ready-made excuses life had handed young Wallenberg, had he wanted to use them to refuse the rescue mission. He was not Jewish, he was rich, he was well-connected politically, he was in line to take the helm of the vast Wallenberg financial empire, and he had everything to lose and nothing to gain by accepting this challenge.

Wallenberg was recommended for this endeavor by Koloman Lauer, a business partner who was involved with the new War Refugee Board. Lauer felt that Raoul possessed the proper combination of dedication, skill, and courage, despite his youth and inexperience, and that his family name would afford him some protection. Wallenberg proved eager to serve, but he boldly demanded and was granted, a great deal of latitude in the methods he would use.

When he learned that Adolf Eichmann was transporting roughly ten to twelve thousand Jews to the gas chambers each day, Wallenberg hastily prepared to travel to Budapest. His "cover" was that of a diplomat, with the official title of First Secretary of the Swedish Legation. He conceived a plan whereby false Swedish passports (Schutzpasse) would be created and used to give potential victims safe passage out of Nazi-controlled territory. In conjunction with this, a series of safe-`houses would be established within Hungary, in the guise of official Swedish legation buildings under diplomatic protection. With this scheme still forming in his mind, "Swedish diplomat" Wallenberg, entered Hungary at the request of the United States War Refugee Board, and his own government on July 6th, 1944, with the mission of saving as many of Hungary's Jews as possible from Nazi liquidation.

He designed the fake passports himself. They were masterpieces, the type of formal, official-appearing pomp which was so impressive to the Nazis. Wallenberg, though young, had traveled and studied extensively abroad, both in the United States (where he attended the University of Michigan as a student of architecture) and in Europe, and he knew how to deal with people and get things done. He worked hard at understanding enemies as well as allies, to know what motivated them; what they admired, what they feared, what they respected. He correctly concluded that the Nazis and Hungarian fascists (Arrow Cross) with whom he would be dealing responded best to absolute authority and official status. He used this principle in fashioning his passports as well as in his personal encounters with the enemy.

Wallenberg began with forty important contacts in Budapest, and quickly cultivated others who were willing to help. It is estimated that under Wallenberg's leadership he and his associates distributed Swedish passports to twenty thousand of Budapest's Jews and protected thirteen thousand more in safe houses, which he rented and over which flew the Swedish flag. However, Eichmann continued to pursue his own mission with fanatical, zealous devotion, and the death camps roared around the clock. Trains packed with people, crammed eighty to a cattle car with nothing but a little water and a bucket for waste, constantly made the four-day journey from Budapest to Auschwitz and back again. The Hungarian countryside was already devoid of Jews, and the situation in the last remaining urban enclaves was critical. And so, Wallenberg himself plunged into the midst of the struggle.

Sandor Ardai was sent by the Jewish underground to drive for Wallenberg. Ardai later told of one occasion when Wallenberg intercepted a trainload of Jews about to leave for Auschwitz. Wallenberg swept past the SS officer who ordered him to depart. In Ardai's words,

"Then he climbed up on the roof of the train and began handing in protective passes through the doors which were not yet sealed. He ignored orders from the Germans for him to get down. Then the Arrow Cross men began shooting and shouting at him to go away. He ignored them and calmly continued handing out passports to the hands that were reaching out for them. I believe the Arrow Cross men deliberately aimed over his head, as not one shot hit him, which would have been impossible otherwise. I think they did this because they were so impressed by his courage. After Wallenberg had handed over the last of the passports, he ordered all those who had one to leave the train and walk to the caravan of cars parked nearby, all marked in Swedish colors. I don't remember exactly how many, but he saved dozens off that train, and the Germans and Arrow Cross were so dumbfounded they let him get away with it!" (Bierman 91)

As the war situation deteriorated for the Germans, Eichmann diverted trains from the death camp routes for more direct use in supplying troops. But all this meant for his victims was that they now had to walk to their destruction. In November, 1944, Eichmann ordered the 125-mile death marches, and the raw elements soon combined with deprivation of food and sleep, turned the roadside from Budapest to the camps, into one massive graveyard. Wallenberg made frequent visits to the stopping areas to do what he could.

In one instance, Wallenberg announced his arrival with all the authority he could muster, and then, "You there!"

The Swede pointed to an astonished man, waiting for his turn to be handed over to the executioner.

"Give me your Swedish passport and get in that line," he barked. "And you get behind him. I know I issued you a passport."

Wallenberg continued, moving fast, talking loud; hoping the authority in his voice would somehow rub off on these defeated people... The Jews finally caught on. They started groping in pockets for bits of identification. A driver's license or birth certificate seemed to do the trick. The Swede was grabbing them so fast; the Nazis, who couldn't read Hungarian anyway, didn't seem to be checking. Faster, Wallenberg's eyes urged them, faster, before the game is up. In minutes he had several hundred people in his convoy. International Red Cross trucks arrived there at Wallenberg's behest, and the Jews clambered on... Wallenberg jumped into his own car.

He leaned out of the car window and whispered, "I am sorry," to the people he was leaving behind. "I am trying to take the youngest ones first," he explained, "I want to save a nation."

This type of action worked many times. Wallenberg and his aides would encounter a death march, and, while Raoul shouted orders for all those with Swedish protective passports to raise their hands, his assistants ran up and down the prisoners' ranks, telling them to raise their hands whether or not they had a document. Wallenberg "then claimed custody of all who had raised their hands and such was his bearing, that none of the Hungarian guards opposed him. The extraordinary thing was the "absolute, convincing power of his behavior," according to Joni Moser.

Wallenberg indirectly helped many who never even saw his face, because as his deeds were talked about, they inspired hope, courage, and action in many people who otherwise felt powerless to escape destruction. He became a symbol of good in a part of the world dominated by evil, and a reminder of the hidden strengths within each human spirit.

Tommy Lapid was thirteen years old in 1944, when he was one of nine hundred people crowded fifteen or twenty to a room in one of the Swedish safe houses. His account illustrates not only vintage Wallenberg tactics, but also how Wallenberg epitomized hope and righteousness, and how his influence extended throughout the land as a beacon to those engulfed in the darkness of despair.

"One morning, a group of these Hungarian Fascists came into the house and said that all the able-bodied women must go with them. We knew what this meant. My mother kissed me and I cried and she cried. We knew we were parting forever and she left me there, an orphan to all intents and purposes. Then, two or three hours later, to my amazement, my mother returned with the other women. It seemed like a mirage, a miracle. My mother was there--she was alive and she was hugging me and kissing me, and she said one word, *"Wallenberg."* I knew who she meant, because Wallenberg was a legend among the Jews. In the complete and total hell in which we lived, there was a savior-angel somewhere, moving around. After she had composed herself, my mother told me that they were being taken to the river when a car arrived and out stepped Wallenberg--and they knew immediately who it was, because there was only one such person in the world. He went up to the Arrow Cross leader and protested that the women were under his protection. They argued with him, but he must have had incredible charisma or some great personal authority, because there was absolutely nothing behind him, no one to back him up. He stood out there in the street, probably feeling like the loneliest man in the world, trying to pretend there was something or someone behind him. They could have shot him then and there in the street and nobody would have known about it. Instead, they relented and let the women go."

Virtually alone in the middle of enemy territory, outnumbered and out-gunned beyond belief, Wallenberg worked miracles on a daily basis. His weapons were courage, self-confidence, ingenuity, understanding of his adversaries, and the ability to inspire others to achieve the goals he set. His leadership was always in evidence. The Nazis and Arrow Cross did not know how to deal with such a man. Here was someone thickly cloaked in apparent authority, but utterly devoid of actual political or military power. Here was a man who was everything they wished they could be in terms of personal strength of character, except for the fact that he was their polar opposite in purpose.

It is impossible to calculate precisely how many people Raoul Wallenberg directly or indirectly saved from certain death. Some estimate the number saved as close to one hundred thousand, and countless more may have survived, in part because of the hope and determination they derived from his leadership and example. (House of Representatives Report, Ninety-Sixth Congress, 2-3). Additionally, he inspired other neutral embassies and the International Red Cross office in Budapest, to join in his efforts to protect the Jews. But the desperate days just prior to the Soviet occupation of Budapest, presented Wallenberg with his greatest challenge and most astonishing triumph.

Eichmann planned to finish the extermination of the remaining one hundred thousand Budapest Jews, in one enormous massacre; if there was no time to ship them to the death camps, he would let their own neighborhoods become their slaughterhouses. To cheat the Allies out of at least part of their victory, he would order some five hundred SS men, and a large number of Arrow Cross, to ring the ghetto and murder the Jews right there. Wallenberg learned of this plot through his network of contacts and tried to intimidate some lower-ranking authorities into backing down, but with the Soviets on their doorsteps, many ceased to care what happened to them. His only hope, and the only hope for the 100,000 surviving Jews, was the overall commander of the SS troops, General August Schmidthuber.

Wallenberg sent a message to Schmidthuber that, if the massacre took place, he would ensure Schmidthuber was held personally responsible and would see him hanged as a war criminal. The bluff worked. The slaughter was called off, and the city fell out of Nazi hands soon thereafter when the Soviet troops rolled in. Thus, tens of thousands were saved in this one incident alone.

But, while peace came to Europe, Wallenberg's fate took a very different path. He vanished, and the whole truth of what happened to him has not been revealed even to this day. From various sources, though, the following seems to have occurred.

The Soviets took Wallenberg into custody when they occupied Budapest, probably because they suspected him of being an anti-Soviet spy. For a decade, they denied any involvement in Wallenberg's disappearance. Then they admitted having incarcerated him, but claimed he died in prison of a heart attack in 1947, when he would have been 35 years old. Since then, however, many people who have served time in Soviet prison have reported seeing Wallenberg, conversing with him, or communicating with him through tap codes. Others have heard of him and his presence in the prisons, but had no direct contact. The Soviets have denied the accuracy of all of these reports and have never deviated from their official position. But in 1989, Soviet officials met with members of Wallenberg's family and turned over some of his personal effects. Reportedly, a genuine investigation was launched in an effort to determine the truth. Whether the years and the prisons will ever yield up their secrets remains to be seen.

In Israel today, there is a grove of trees planted by the Martyrs' and Heroes' Remembrance Authority, or *Yad Vashem. Known as *The Avenue of the Righteous,* each tree memorializes a "righteous Gentile," someone who risked his or her life to help Jews during the Holocaust. The trees stand in silent testament to those who, in the words of a former speaker of Israel's parliament, "saved not only the Jews but the honor of Man". Along with Raoul Wallenberg's tree, there is a medal. His medal bears the language of the Talmud and summarizes his mission in the words,

"Whoever saves a single soul, it is as if he had saved the whole world."

The chairman of *Yad Vashem,* Gideon Hausner, who also prosecuted Adolf Eichmann, summarized his feelings for Raoul Wallenberg in this way:

> "There is much we all can learn from Raoul Wallenberg's leadership. His courage came from caring for others, hoping for their success and not his own. He demonstrated both moral and physical courage because he had a choice, he was not forced into the situation; he chose to be a part of it."

As a leader, Wallenberg was out front, not in the corporate offices or behind the wealth of his family. He showed courage and sincerity. He responded to an obvious need with imagination and creativity. He would not want today's generation to feel sorry for him, I am sure he knew, he understood what was involved and he fully accepted the consequences.

Finally, he knew himself. He had a grasp of his talents and weaknesses and how they fit in with his purpose and goals. Thus, what he could not possibly have accomplished through military force or physical violence, he did through bravado, intimidation, and illusion. Any other tactics would have met with crushing defeat. This is not to imply that leaders should always behave in this manner. It simply suggests that these strategies employed by Wallenberg, were essential to fulfill his objective under the most extraordinary of conditions, and that they were chosen with full comprehension of the alternatives and their consequences. But most importantly, his motive was pure, it was not for selfish gratification and gain; it was because he saw the Jews as his friends.

Becoming a mature leader means first becoming yourself, learning who you are and what you stand for. Implicit in this notion is the theory of self-discovery, getting in touch with oneself. Wallenberg teaches us that to grow as a leader involves reflecting on oneself, putting values in perspective, thinking about the task to be accomplished, and influencing and motivating others to get the job done.

Wallenberg's work in Hungary is a testimony that leaders are foot soldiers who battle for the ideals in which they believe, and that leadership has far less to do with using other people than with serving other people.

Selfless service is the key to successful leadership, which in turn can result in meaningful accomplishments. Raoul Wallenberg found himself and the meaning of his life, by losing it in the service of others.

The process of learning about oneself and others, on an in-depth level, requires hard work. It is not something that can be gained solely from book study. It evolves best through personal introspection, human interaction and feedback, and through life experiences, observations, and analysis.

It involves large quantities of common sense and realistic perspective. But its yield is high; it pays big dividends to those leaders who spend the time and make the extra effort to go beneath the surface, to discover what makes a person tick; because life and its activities are all part of the human experience. Bottom line; it is all a matter of people, and the leader who understands people, understands leadership.

Wallenberg's work in Hungary demonstrates that effective leadership is neither neutral nor sterile. It is deeply emotional, and leaders cannot set aside the individual and their needs, and have a deeply felt belief in the worth of those who follow them; not merely a casual sense of, "it's only a job". Total commitment comes only from total conviction that the people we serve are significant to the organization.

Not too long ago, a department manager, Jack Chaney, whom I deeply respected came to me, and asked if it was okay to invite his department to his home for a Christmas Party. He had been told by his immediate supervisor that it was considered fraternization, and he shouldn't do it. As the top HR executive, I assured him that not only was it okay, but if kept within the realms of decency and sincere social bonding, it would improve his team's performance and respect for each other. When I left the organization, Jack was the most respected leader there, and his employees were known for their commitment and excellent performance.

If valuing an individual's friendship by a leader is seen as only relative by the organization; if there is no right and wrong; if one system of government is morally equivalent to all others; then there is nothing worth sacrificing for. The leader will be limited to appeal to local pride and self-interest, in an attempt to inspire excellence. The result will often be halfhearted effort--and failure.

Leaders are not afraid to do the unexpected

Throughout his entire experience in Hungary, in all that he did, Wallenberg had the daring to accept himself as a bundle of possibilities. He boldly undertook the game of making the most of his best. Wallenberg instructs us that the leader is not a superman, but simply a fully functioning human being. Successful leaders are aware of their possibilities and do not let self ambition to please others or to build up ones own pride, take over. Such leaders become afraid to take risks and are afraid to do the unexpected.

Erich Fromm said that the pity in life today is that most of us die before we are fully born. Leaders such as Wallenberg are not merely observers of life, but active participants. They take the calculated risks required to exercise leadership, and experiment with the untried. It is surprising (and most aspiring leaders do not realize it), but much failure comes from people literally standing in their own way, preventing their own progress. Wallenberg never blocked his own path; rather, he created new paths where others saw only impenetrable walls. In the process, he was able to motivate others to do the same. He was a dispenser of hope in an environment filled with hopelessness and despair.

History is replete with instances where small, militarily weaker forces triumphed on the strength of superior strategy and tactics. Ingenuity makes surprise possible and allows quick adaptation and reaction to an adversary's actions. Without flexibility, humans are reduced to automatons, programmed only for failure.

Ingenuity requires information as its fuel. The established objective and the available tools and procedures provide the raw material for any leadership action. But much can be accomplished when leaders reach beyond traditional methods and use the status quo as a floor rather than a ceiling. Leaders must be evaluated on the basis of what they achieve. Results are what count, not formulaic adherence to precedent.

Leaders must be achievers and result-oriented. We can "do more with less" when we allow, and encourage our followers to think creatively, and not confine them to what has already been done. Military leaders are often criticized for preparing to fight the *previous* war. The best leaders think of all the possible ways in which available resources might be used or modified to achieve the objective, and expect those under them to participate, creating a group thought.

Few leaders will ever have the opportunity to help as many people as did Raoul Wallenberg. Still, each victory is immeasurably precious for those whose futures are impacted at the plants, the offices, schools, wherever our leadership shadow may fall. They, their children, their grandchildren, their entire posterity, and all whose lives are and will be touched by you, owe their existence to that one heartbeat of time when a leader took action, despite the dangers or loss of career. Although conditions may differ, the lessons for leadership should be valuable for all who aspire to more effective leadership. With patient application, it can be transferred and applied to everyday leadership problems, whether on the level of CEO's or individuals.

"Whoever has a positive impact on a single soul, it is as if he had impacted the whole world."

The following is an excerpt from USA Today, Thursday, March 21, 1991

> **WALLENBERG CASE:** The Soviet Union handed Sweden, seventy hitherto secret documents on the case of missing, Swedish diplomat, Raoul Wallenberg. Wallenberg, who saved thousands of Hungarian Jews from Nazi death camps, disappeared after Soviet troops entered Budapest in the last days of World War II. Swedish radio and the documents, reportedly confirm a Soviet claim that Wallenberg died of a heart attack in a Moscow prison in 1947.

Leaders have Moral Courage

"To know what is right and not do it is cowardice."

In history, we find many examples of leaders with true physical courage; but what example do we have of true moral courage? Consider the example of General Doniphan, an obscure frontier Missouri militia general, who rose from being a school teacher to a heroic figure, because of his courage to do the right things during unpopular times.

"**Nearly all men can stand adversity, but if you want to test a man's character, give him power." Abraham Lincoln**

Case of Courage – The Doniphan Story

On November 1st, 1838, during the Mormon War, Missouri Militia Commander, General Lucas, ordered Mormon leaders, Joseph Smith and some followers, to be brought into the Missouri Militia's camp to be tried by a court-martial. The charges were treason. It appears rumors had spread against the religious group that they were conspiring to overthrow the government and kill Governor Boggs, the Governor of Missouri.

The charges were completely without merit, but the public opinion was against the Mormons. Joseph Smith knew that many innocent lives would be taken if a full out war were to be conducted. He brought all the Mormon leaders together and a decision was made to pursue peace talks with the Missouri officials. Surrendering himself to the authorities, Joseph Smith was taken to stand before his accusers who were composed "of nineteen militia officers, and seventeen preachers of various sects, who had served as volunteers against the Mormons."

The trial was brief, and Joseph Smith and his associates were condemned to be shot in the public square of Far West Missouri, in the presence of their families and friends! General Doniphan, as brigadier general of the state militia, was ordered by General Lucas to execute them. General Doniphan flatly refused to carry out the orders.

General Doniphan opposed the decision of the court-martial to shoot Joseph and the other Mormon leaders. Due to his firmness and the determination that neither he, nor his brigade, should take part in "a cold-blooded murder," the lives of the Mormon leaders were spared.

General Doniphan was true to himself not only during this incident with the Mormon leader, but throughout his life. His moral courage at any time, could have cost him his political career, including the financial repercussions against him. In a rare display of both physical and moral courage, General Doniphan knew the price for refusing to carry out the extermination order, could be costly.

Did General Doniphan struggle with his decision? He left no records or journals behind for us to know, but I am sure he struggled; it's human. What we do know is what resulted from his actions.

Not all acts of courage bring such spectacular rewards. But all of them do bring peace and contentment; just as cowardice, in the end, always brings regret and remorse.

Courage Becomes Easier Once it's Practiced

I know that from my own experience as a Second Lieutenant stationed on the DMZ in Korea, I struggled with my own actions as a emerging officer. One of my first struggles with courage came as I witnessed a rather brutal act on a member of my platoon by my Company Commander. The Captain became angry at a soldier and threw a gas mask hitting the soldier in the face, followed by verbal abuse and humiliation; while I stood by and did nothing. The soldier was helpless. He knew that if he were to retaliate, he faced severe punishment, to include possible jail time; but I could see the anger inside him fueled by the humiliation of the act. Later that night, the incident weighed heavily on my mind and I couldn't sleep. As I was contemplating the event, I was somewhat ashamed of my inaction. I had let the fear of loosing my career impact another person, but most importantly, a member of my platoon who had an element of trust in my position as his leader. I felt that his trust in me had been rightfully compromised. I was sure that not only he, but other members of the group whom I led, had lost trust in me to protect them.

During this deep period of reflection, SSG Evans, a squad leader and friend, came up to me, placed his hand on my shoulder and said, "Lieutenant, don't ever be afraid to stand up for what is right."

His words sunk deep into my conscious. For years afterwards, I worried because I didn't have the courage to stand up to the Captain, but I resolved to never lose courage again when it came to principle and people.

Years later while stationed in Panama, I faced another incident which would test my courage, as a Captain in command of a joint task force. My mission was to escort three, U.S. Army Landing Craft (LCM), up the Gulf of Darien, to a forward operations base commanded by the Panamanians in the remote jungle town of El Real, between Panama and Columbia. We were to provide ammunition and medical supplies to the Panamanian Defense Force

(PDF) conducting drug raids against the Columbian Cartels.

General Manuel Noriega, then dictator of Panama, had appointed one of his officers to accompany our task force. His name was **Major Giroldi. Our boat LCM commander was a bright and lively U.S. Army Transportation Lieutenant. As the task force commander, I was responsible for the group and getting the supplies to the joint task force at El Real. The first part of the trip was uneventful. We departed the Panama Canal Zone into the Pacific ocean, following the coastline to the Gulf of Darien. The PDF Major spent most of his time sleeping on our upper deck near the wheel house. As we approached the estuary for the final trip up the swollen muddy river to El Real, the Major became alive and began to take command; that is, he cursed and intimidated the soldiers on the boat. He berated them, focusing on the young Lieutenant harder than the others, claiming they were soft and could never serve under a Panamanian Officer.

After about ten minutes, I had heard enough. I stepped over and stood nose to nose with the Major and demanded that he stop his tirades, that it was not necessary, and if he had problems to direct them to me.

For a while it seemed to calm him down. As we approached the base, he must have felt a strong need to, once more, show his power and authority. In a near frenzy-like action, he started throwing ropes at the soldiers, barking commands, cursing. Then he grabbed the Lieutenant by the shirt and started to walk to the front of the open ramp. Instinctively, I stepped in front of the Major.

While his crew looked on, I pulled the Lieutenant away from his hold, ordered the boat to stop and said, "Major Giroldi, I don't know what you are doing but as long as I am here, you will never touch or yell at these men again. I am turning these boats around right now – you can come with us or I will drop you off at the shore, which will it be?"

There was a blistering moment of silence; his brown eyes pierced my soul. "What is it to be," I demanded.

Nothing – just his dead glare at me.

"Okay, Lieutenant, take the boat to El Real, we are going to drop the Major off and return down river."

We dropped Major Giroldi and his group off at El Real and returned down

**Note: During Operation Just Cause – On October 3, 1989. A coup attempt against General Noriega instigated by Major Giroldi failed. Maj. Giroldi was summarily executed by General Noriega after the General failed to convince the Major to commit suicide.

river. My final view of the Major was of him waving his hands, walking towards the operations center. A short distance down the river and around the bend, I had the boats drop anchor and radioed our situation to the 193rd Infantry Brigade Tactical Operations Center, located at Ft. Clayton, Panama.

There were minor consequences to my actions due to the political nature of our operation, but I also had a great deal of support. It had been a risky decision, but the right one in my mind. It was a decision that tested a personal commitment I had made to myself years before. I had made a promise never to allow my fears and self interest to hurt others. I was a leader, who had impact on others. If they could not trust me to protect them, who could they trust?

"Leaders do not react to fear, they act on the principles of right and wrong."

We fulfilled our mission and I returned to El Real that night. I never saw Major Giroldi again, but the lesson was driven home. Leadership requires courage and risk; the hardest being moral courage. Since that incident, I have never experienced failed courage. The truth is that once you have stepped up, it is easy afterwards. Having courage feels good. I learned this one principle:

Doing nothing wrong is not the same as doing the right thing

Courage becomes easier as we learn to drive our fears out and our convictions in. Decisions become better and those around us respect who we are.

Several years later I had the chance to work with U.S. Rep. Ike Skelton (D-MO), from Missouri. Representative Skelton was in Panama to gather facts concerning the role and future of the famous School of Americas, which at that time was located in Panama. It was a school designed to train foreign officers from around Central and South America in counter-insurgency, irregular warfare, psychological-operations, and combat arms orientation.

On one of our trips together, I had the opportunity to ask him a few questions that had been on my mind. I asked him what he felt was the most important thing he did as a United States Representative?

Without hesitation the answer came, "Taking care of people".

I then asked another question.

"What is the most important characteristic a leader needs as a Senator, Congressman, or an Army Officer?"

To my delight and without hesitation, his answer was, "Courage".

He was not referring to physical courage, but rather moral courage. Having the courage to take care of the individual is not always popular or easy as a politician, especially when special interest groups launch artful media attacks against you, when they don't get their way, or where opponents are always looking for cracks in your armor.

Senator Skelton shared with me several incidents from his life that also had impact on him and helped to define his courage; specifically as a member of the Armed Services Committee, issues and situations he faced that challenged his moral courage. To this day, I have not met a leader with such sincerity, whose very actions speak for themselves.

At the end of our discussion, he made the comment, "Captain Shelton, more than anytime in our military history, we need men and women of character and courage," and then with a pause, he declared, "We need men and women who understand sacrifice, I am afraid that money and things have robbed us of that."

Leaders are afraid to sacrifice when it is most needed. My takeaway from Ike Skelton was:

Anything worthwhile in life has an element of sacrifice.

Over the years, I have learned to respond to the whisperings of my conscience. I have lived my life in such a way, that I can listen to those internal promptings and have the courage to do as it instructs. Of course I have continued to face fear, experience ridicule, and meet opposition. The difference is that I have the courage to defy the consensus; the courage to stand for principle.

A moral coward is one who is afraid to do what he thinks is right, because others will disapprove or laugh. Remember, all men have their fears, but those who face their fears with dignity have courage.

As leaders, you are regularly required to make choices on the basis of what you know to be right. We are free in most instances, to make our own decisions, but we are never free to determine the final outcomes of our choices.

It is not enough for us to know what is right and to believe it is good. We must be willing to stand up and be counted. We must be willing to act in accordance with what we believe under all circumstances. It is of little value for us to believe one way if we behave contrary to that belief in our private actions, or in our business performance. Today, it requires great courage to be an effective leader. For many it is not easy, and it will likely not become easier. The tests of our day are severe. This is particularly so for young, emerging leaders.

Being true to correct leadership principles does not always make us popular, but I can almost guarantee it will be admired. Having the courage of our convictions has its own rewards. It brings satisfaction and fulfillment into our lives, rather than discouragement and defeat. As a leader you do not want to ever have the heavy weight of regret on your shoulders.

The nature of the challenges we face as leaders is not nearly as important as what we choose to do about them. When we have the courage to live up to the best we know, we fulfill the purpose for which we came to this earth, and we provide an incentive for others to do the same.

EXERCISE

Think of a time in your career or life where you lacked courage to act.

1.What was the root cause of your inaction?

2.What would you do differently if a similar action were to happen to-day?

POINTS OF DISCUSSION

What did General Doniphan and Raoul Wallenberg have in common?

Why did they take such risks?

What type of courage did they demonstrate most, physical or moral?

What were the underlying characteristics of Major Giroldi, General Lucas, and Adolf Eichmann?

8

BEING OFFENDED

Choose Not to Be Offended

I have seen good leaders become poor decision makers as result of being offended. As leaders, when we believe or say we have been offended, we usually mean we feel insulted, mistreated, snubbed, or disrespected. Certainly clumsy, embarrassing, unprincipled, and mean-spirited things do occur in our interactions with other people at work, at home and at social gatherings, which would allow us to take offense. However, as leaders you can not allow those above you or who work for you, to offend you. We make the choice to be offended, thus submitting ourselves to poor decision making, and leaving ourselves open to poor judgment. Nothing clouds a leader's decision making more than allowing offense to enter into making decisions. Effective leaders understand this one principle:

"To be offended is a *choice* we make; it is not a *condition* inflicted or imposed upon us by someone or something else." *Dr. David Allen Bednar*

As leaders, we have moral agency...the capacity for independent action and choice. Our ability to make choices requires leaders to act, and not just be acted upon. As a leader, to believe that our superior or a follower can *make* us feel offended, angry, hurt, or bitter, diminishes our ability to control our decision making, and transforms us into ineffective leaders to be acted upon. As leaders, you have the power to act and to choose how you will respond to an offense.

On many occasions during the civil war, President Lincoln elected not to be offended. In one example during the early years of the civil war, Lincoln went to the residence of General Grant to discuss the poor performance of his army. Lincoln waited several hours for the general to arrive home. When Grant arrived, he was informed that the President was waiting. For unknown reasons, Grant chose to ignore the President, going directly to his bedroom without visiting with Lincoln retiring for the night. When finally informed that Grant had retired to bed, the President responded by suggesting, "the General had a lot on his mind, and probably needed the rest." Lincoln did not let the offense act on him; he maintained control of the otherwise tense situation. Lincoln mastered the principle of not becoming offended. This characteristic may very well have been the key to his ability to make good decisions.

In many instances, choosing to be offended is a symptom of a much deeper and more serious problem for leaders, who may be insecure with their leadership. An example is that of Benedict Arnold, who was a personal favorite and friend of George Washington. Arnold, who had been a successful field commander under Washington, was brilliant in the field; however his pride and inability to handle offenses caused him to loose everything. Arnold's downfall began as a number of junior officers received promotions to Brigadier General above him, leaving him behind. He became offended. Arnold would go on to win major battles against the British and was promoted with his seniority restored; but he was already too angry to forgive Congress, and never would.

By May of 1779, Arnold made contact with the British to hand over the defense plans of West Point. Why would a man commit treason against his country, especially one who had fought so valiantly? He was offended, angry, and hurt over the many slights he received over the years. He felt unappreciated by his country and those he fought with, even sacrificing his own leg for the cause. His pride was most likely the biggest part of his life that was damaged — humiliation was always an affront Arnold could never take. Money, of course, played a big part. He was offered in excess of 10,000 pounds and a commission in the British military.

The British provided handsomely for Arnold, but never completely trusted him. He was never given an important military command. He and his wife moved to London, where he found no job, some admiration, and some contempt. He eventually moved his family to Canada, where he reentered the shipping business. The Tories there disliked him and had no use for him, and eventually he returned his family to London. When the fighting began between France and England, he tried again for military service, but to no avail. His shipping ventures eventually failed and he died in 1801, virtually unknown, his wife joining him in death three years later.

Arnold allowed himself to be acted upon, and the eventual results were betrayal to his country and misery. Compare to Abraham Lincoln, who was a leader who exercised his agency and acted in accordance with effective leadership principles of not being offended; Lincoln became a mighty instrument in American history.

The capacity to conquer offense may seem beyond most leaders reach. This capability, however, is not reserved for, or restricted to, prominent leaders; it can and should be exercised at every level of leadership down even to the front-line supervisor and manager.

Perfecting our ability to avoid the pitfalls of being offended, I would suggest that we will spend our entire life learning how to lead without being offended. Every position we attain is a learning laboratory, and a workshop in which we gain experience as we practice the ongoing process of perfecting our leadership.

An inexperienced leader learns valuable lessons as he leads both supportive as well as non-supportive followers, and thereby becomes a more effective leader. A new or young leader learns how to be a leader through experience, and by working with other leaders and followers who wholeheartedly support him, even while recognizing his inexperience.

Understanding that the workplace is a learning laboratory helps us to prepare for an inevitable reality. In some way and at some time, someone in the workplace will do or say something that could be considered offensive. Such an event will surely happen to each and every one of us—and it certainly will occur more than once. Much of how we are respected and viewed as leaders will depend on how we react to those offenses.

You and I cannot control the intentions or behavior of other people. However, we do determine how we will act. Remember that as leaders, you and I are free to make choices and we can choose not to be offended. An option that is not acceptable is for a leader to get even.

An old Chinese proverb states:

"If you are going to kill a man, dig two graves, one for you and one for the other"

Chinese Proverb – Author Unknown

Example from the First Iraq War

A more current example of this leadership principle was seen during the first Iraq war. An exchange of words and communications occurred between General Norman Schwarzkopf, and Colon Powell, the Secretary of Defense. General Schwarzkopf, whose army was suffering because of inadequate logistical support, had a sharp exchange of words with Powell, by the way of condemnation and criticism that accused Powell of thoughtlessness, slothfulness, and neglect. Powell might easily have resented Schwarzkopf and his message, but he chose not to take offense. Powell responded compassionately, and described how Congress was divided in how to deploy the troops and equipment of which Schwarzkopf was not aware.

Powell responded, "I know you are under a lot of pressure and it bothers me that we can't act quicker, you're criticism is understood. I am not mad, but am glad to have a general of your caliber heading the Army."

One of the greatest indicators of our own leadership maturity is revealed in how we respond to the weaknesses, the inexperience, and the potentially offensive actions of others. A thing, an event, or an expression may be offensive, but you and I can choose not to be offended, and to say with General Powell, "I am not mad or angry."

Clearly, the rigorous requirements that lead to effective leadership for you, includes experiences that test and challenge us. If a follower says or does something that we consider offensive, our first obligation is to refuse to take offense and then communicate privately, honestly, and directly with that individual. Such an approach builds trust, respect, and permits misperceptions to be clarified leaving true intent to be understood.

Case of Reacting vs. Acting

While serving as the Director of Human Resources for Vlasic International, I had an experience that taught me a great leadership lesson regarding being offended as a front-line leader. I was preparing a disciplinary action against a supervisor who had been with the organization for over ten years. The supervisor had been charged with verbally abusing one of his workers, and was facing termination because of his actions.

I asked him what led him to use fowl and abusive language. He shared his story with me. While starting daily operations, one of his more vocal employees made a sarcastic and disrespectful remark to a fellow worker regarding him. It was equally as vulgar, and the supervisor had heard the comments.

When he approached the employee regarding the remarks, the employee became disrespectful again, intensifying the supervisors anger. The supervisor asked himself, *what have I done to deserve this?*

Unfortunately, the supervisor reacted with a verbal string of language that was personal and racial. As I listened to the supervisor, I remembered the leadership principle on the importance of acting instead of reacting, to the events around us. The supervisor had made a fundamental mistake by reacting.

I asked him why he did not pull the employee aside and act. I told him that an appropriate action was to ask the employee, "Help me understand why you made the comments that you did?" He had no answer. The problem was he failed to act rather than react.

That experience demonstrated for me that in most encounters, leaders can determine the kind of experience they are going to have by how they respond. It was tragic that this supervisor reacted the way he did, it not only cost him his job, but the negative impact to the organization in lost talent and loss of trust for management was costly.

In today's fast-paced business world, there seems to be a greater tendency for people to act aggressively toward each other. Some are quick to take offense, and respond angrily to real or imagined affronts, and we've all experienced or heard reports of managers who fly into rages, or other examples of rude, insensitive behavior, that undermine a leader's respect and trust with followers.

Leaders who struggle with unbalanced aggressiveness can learn a lesson from Viktor Frank. Reflecting on his horrendous, wartime experiences, Viktor Frank recalled: "We, who lived in concentration camps, can remember the men who walked through the huts comforting others, giving away their last piece of bread. They may have been few in number, but they offer sufficient proof that everything can be taken from a man but one thing: the last of the human freedoms—*to choose one's attitude in any given set of circumstances, is to choose one's own way.*"

As front-line leaders who have power and authority, it is in the workplace that our behavior is most significant. It is the place where our actions have the greatest impact. Sometimes we are so filled with power, pride, or ego that we no longer guard our words or our actions. We forget simple civility. If we are not on guard, we can fall into the habit of criticizing, losing our tempers, or behaving selfishly.

When leaders become offended and demonstrate that offense through power and abuse, employees may be quick to forgive because they work for them, have an implied obligation, or because of job security; but they often carry away, in silence, unseen injuries and unspoken resentment towards the leader.

There are too many workplaces where workers fear their leaders because of their reactions to perceived offenses. This fear leads to the fostering of a work environment and atmosphere of contention, conflict, and contempt in the workplace. It diminishes any trust or respect that workers may have for those leaders.

Leaders must set the example of maintaining emotional control in every setting, and not let offense control their actions. In the face of criticism and implications, the leader must maintain his composure, refusing to act unkindly or disrespectfully.

Many leaders, who most need to hear this message about choosing not to be offended, are probably not reading this or any other, like literature. We all have met them, and have seen the affects of leaders who have been offended and the actions that followed. If you have a problem with this principle, work hard to control it and be not offended.

POINTS OF DISCUSSION

Do you feel that allowing yourself to be offended is a weakness? Why or Why not?

Make a list of reasons why you have been offended in the past and how you reacted to the offenses.

What could you do in the future to avoid being offended or how would you react?

How did Abraham Lincoln and Collin Powell handle offenses?

CONCLUSION

True Case Study – When Leaders Really Don't Care

I was working at a meat processing plant when I met Samuel Houston a clean-up worker in our sanitation department. At first, I knew Sam only as an African American, 52 year old employee who kept mostly to himself and was at work every day. I would occasionally say "Hi" to him as I walked around the plant on a daily basis, but it wasn't until a snowy day in December that I really knew who Sam Houston was. That day, Sam had called in to work, asking if someone could pick him up. The snow had stopped all public transportation in the area and only a few workers were making it in. I jumped into my pickup and drove a few miles to where Sam lived in a simple row home by himself.

Our drive back to the plant was enjoyable, Sam shared with me stories from his life, his travels, his family and his work experience; I really got to know Sam. Sam shared with me his accomplishments and his struggles, he had family, hobbies, a life and above all many dreams yet unfulfilled. He was a charming man with a great mind and many talents.

At work however, age had caught up with Sam and he wasn't as fast as in years past, but his work ethic and dedication was strong. Sam had worked at the plant for one year and seemed happy with what he was doing. After I dropped Sam off at work, I checked on him frequently, our greetings were different, more caring and genuine. We became good friends, I would do anything I could to help Sam and ensure he was doing OK.

Several months later our company had a recall of product; management reacted harshly and demanded action. Unfortunately some managers started pointing fingers; one of those fingers landed upon the shoulders of Sam Houston. The allegations against Sam included; not adequately cleaning the large totes that the meat went into, causing deadly bacteria to grow that in turn contributed to the recall of product. Sam's supervisor came to me with the intentions of firing Sam for the negligence. I asked the supervisor to lay out the findings and reasons for terminating Sam. Sam's supervisor returned with a long list, among the reasons were; he doesn't do what we ask him to do, he is intimidating, he resists change, he's slow, and most of all, he is hard to work with.

After reviewing the charges and documentation, I told the supervisor that I would not support Sam's termination; I felt that he had not done enough to help Sam identify and correct the problems. For the moment Sam was saved, the supervisor stormed away and I knew at that point that Sam Houston was gone. The supervisor would start the cycle of Self Fulfilling Prophecy where the loser is always the employee. Eventually Sam was fired, he left devastated and demoralized, his self esteem had been destroyed. His failure was the failure of the system and the team that he was part of.

The day Samuel Houston left the company, the company lost a good employee and I lost the benefit of a good friend. What caused Sam to fail? Let me list them for you:

1. Communications
2. Lack of regular feedback
3. No accountability until it was too late
4. Never a positive word of encouragement
5. Selfishness
6. Using fear to lead
7. The supervisor was afraid for his own job
8. Untrained and ineffective leadership
9. Inability to motivate
10. Seeking for and finding blame
11. Failure to become a friend – guarding the individuals interest
12. Lack of moral courage to accept responsibility

13. Lack of team building

14. Lack of benevolence

In many ways Sam Houston's case defines leadership incompetence; it is the American business tragedy and is the by-product of poor training, not caring and the absence of good leadership. Unfortunately I could not save Sam from his fate because it was sealed the day his leaders failed to see him as a valuable asset.

HISTORICAL LEADERS

Jesus Christ Abraham Lincoln Mahatma Gandhi	Adolph Hitler Joseph Stalin Saddam Hussein Omar Al-Bashar Kim Jong-Il
Impact on mankind – Positive	Impact on mankind – Negative
Selfless	Selfish
Concerned with freedom	Concerned with control
Concerned with service	Concerned with status
Met the genuine needs of others	Concerned with only their needs and wants
Concerned with others development and progress	Sought to manipulate others
Led with compassion balanced by justice	Led with harshness and injustice

DESIRABLE LEADERSHIP QUALITIES TEST
THE MAN IN THE MIRROR

Ask yourself this question each time for each point. "Am I truly _____,"
(using placing each characteristic in the blank.) Then, *mentally*, look into
the mirror, the person in the mirror is the best judge. Answer yes or no.

	Am I	
	YES	**NO**
Trusted	_____	_____
Competent	_____	_____
Understanding	_____	_____
Open-Minded	_____	_____
Dedicated	_____	_____
Caring	_____	_____
Trustworthy	_____	_____
Responsible	_____	_____
Flexible	_____	_____
Disciplined	_____	_____
Cooperative	_____	_____
Believable	_____	_____
Concern for others	_____	_____
Loyal	_____	_____
Totals	_____	_____

There are arguments that some of these characteristics are too ambiguous and that there are degrees of competencies. I would argue this – You Know -. You either are or you have struggled with one or all. Answer it without debate; give it your unbiased true view. Remember: You know.

No one is perfect, nor will we be, but we can stretch ourselves to reach perfection and improve on these characteristics so that we become meaningful to others. Knowing your weaknesses and acting to improve them takes courage. Knowing your weaknesses and doing nothing to improve is arrogance.

DEDICATION

To my mother who always believed in me and always gave me encouraging words. Her unwavering faith and example has been my standard. Her gift of kindness and understanding has been my guide.

To my father who set the example and whose wisdom is reflected in these pages. His greatest gift to me has been his unquestionable integrity and enduring work ethic.

To my brother who defines the meaning of ambition and whose example I shall always treasure. His unquestionable faith and commitment has always been an example for me and my family.

To my son-in law and our grandson, Obadiah Sr and Jr. You represent the hope of the future and strength of family.

To my five children who have always rallied around me when times were difficult and provided much comfort and joy. Each brings uniqueness and blessings that always has been appreciated and admired.

To my wife Suzanne, my best friend of over 30 years, she has always been my biggest fan and supporter. Without her unwavering strength, my accomplishments would be few and my happiness fleeting.

Leadership is all about serving others

Someone asked me which of my five children my favorite was. My reply: My favorite child is the one who is sick until he or she gets well or the one who is absent until they return.

I have spent more than 15 years working with the Hispanic immigrant population in meat processing plants, manufacturing and within the community. I have shared their dinner tables, visited the sick, attended funerals and have been a guest at their celebrations. I have visited their husbands in jail during U.S. government-sponsored Operation South PAW (Protecting American Workers) in September 1995 and took over 15 families, mostly young children and wives, to Little Rock Arkansas to visit their fathers being held in federal detention. To these families and the estimated 14 million immigrants, I dedicate this page to them by means of the following public address I gave in December 2006, at a gathering for a major meat processing company.

Dedicated to the First Generation Hispanic Immigrant – Speech

Being a first-generation Hispanic immigrant is not always easy. You will walk where no one in your family has walked before. Conditions around you may be challenging. You may have few, or no, friends or relatives to understand and support you. At times you may become discouraged, wondering if it is all worth it. All first-generation immigrants occupy a special and important place in the history of the United States of America and their families.

You add great strength to the country you are in with your, talents, abilities, and energy to build the economy where you are. Most of you reach out in kindness to those around you, lifting and helping them through difficult times. So much of what is done in the industries you serve at today could not be done without your efforts.

More importantly, as a first-generation immigrant, you occupy an important place in your family. You are an example to your family of sacrifice and dedication. Whether they are with you or not, as you work hard in this country, those around you will feel the sacrifice and dedication to hard work through you. Those who are not immigrants know that you are engaged in something different and special, even if they do not understand it or have enough knowledge to accept it. I can assure you that history will speak kindly of you and your sacrifices; and to those who oppose you; future generations who read about your struggles and challenges, will chastise your tormentors for their hardness and intolerance.

Resist the poison of bitterness and anger, for its venom will reach your children and affect them. Be patient and kind, work hard each day to know how you can become good citizens. Those patterns will shape your life, but more importantly, they will become a standard for your family and posterity.

ABOUT THE AUTHOR

Dr. Ed Shelton is an experienced, business executive who is a top speaker and presenter. Few businessmen have the depth and understanding of the front line workers and those who lead them than what Dr. Shelton offers. His friends and business colleagues describe him as a modern day champion of the American worker who has dedicated his life to building front line leaders.

Dr. Shelton's experiences bring leadership examples to light in a way that is entertaining and real. He is unique in that he has studied leadership as a military officer, an assistant professor, a senior executive in manufacturing and meat processing and from the lens as a civic leader within his community.

Leadership experiences in the military include serving as an Infantry Platoon Leader on the DMZ in Korea and two tours as an Infantry Company Commander in Panama and in the U.S. His leadership training included attendance at the Infantry Officer Basic and Advanced Course at Ft. Benning Georgia, Chilean War Academy in Santiago Chili, U.S. Army Airborne School, Jungle Warfare School, and Special Operations School in Hurlburt Field Florida. Dr. Shelton's military decorations include the U.S. Army Parachutist Badge, Expert Infantry Badge, and Meritorious Service Medal with oak leaf cluster. Other distinguished awards included the Artillery Saint Barbara Medal.

As Assistant Professor at Penn State University, Dr. Shelton developed and taught leadership courses that included leadership building, training model for young emerging leaders and skills based training programs.

His research in Hispanic immigrant labor is regarded as essential literature in meat and poultry organizations and in cultural leadership development.

Dr. Shelton's greatest contribution has been in industry and meat processing plants throughout the United States. Working as an executive in organizations such as Simmons Foods, Excell Beef Company (Cargil Meat Solutions), Vlasic International, Smithfield Foods, Fleetwood Homes of Texas and Bar-S Foods. Dr. Shelton has developed and implemented leadership programs that have been effective in union avoidance campaigns and used by employees to decertify unions. His expertise and programs have elevated many plants to best overall status within their organizations.

Dr. Shelton has lived in Germany, Italy, Korea, and Panama and in the U.S., Oklahoma, Texas, Missouri, Florida, Pennsylvania, Ohio, North Carolina and Colorado. He has a ranch home near Waco Texas where he resides with his wife Suzanne Shelton an English High School teacher and his five children; Crystal, Charmaine, Samuel, Annette and Barbara. His greatest happiness has been his marriage to Suzanne for over 30 years.

Dr. Shelton's ambitious nature and fascination with leadership manifests itself in his personal interests. He has raised five children, is a certified PADI Scuba Diving Instructor, a licensed FAA Single Engine pilot, and is an acclaimed expedition leader to the San Blas Region of Caledonia Bay.

PHOTO'S

3rd Platoon A Company DMZ Korea – Author is center Left seated on box.

A Company – Camp liberty Bell Korea

SSG Evans – 1979 DMZ Korea

SSG Evans center right and SSG Swain far right

Captain Shelton – El Real forward base along Columbian border

Captain Shelton far right standing at the War College, Santiago Chili

Dr. Shelton with Senator Ike Skelton, School of Americas, Panama

Penn State Students at Leadership Development – Caledonia Bay Exercise

Penn State Students – Caledonia Bay Leadership Exercise – Author in background

SUPERVISOR POCKET GUIDE FROM LEADERSHIP DESIGN:

Dr. EDWARD J. SHELTON
The Leadership Book

Dr. Shelton shares important leadership ideas and thoughts in this condensed pocket sized book. Perfect for front line supervisors, its laminated pages are designed for the working environment. The Leadership Book puts focus on influence, motivation, commitment and trust.

To order this book, call (254) 624-8999